£3

EMOTIONAL

HEALTH

By the same Author:

Homoeopathic Medicine (Thorsons)

The Homoeopathic Treatment of Emotional Illness (Thorsons)

A Woman's Guide to Homoeopathy (Thorsons)

Understanding Homoeopathy (Insight)

An Encyclopaedia of Homoeopathy (Insight)

The Principles, Art and Practise of Homoeopathy (Insight)

Personal Growth and Creativity(Insight)

EMOTIONAL

HEALTH

Dr Trevor Smith
M.A., M.B., B. Chir., D.P.M., M.F.Hom

INSIGHT

Insight Edition

WORTHING Sussex

Insight edition first published 1986

© Insight Editions 1986

British Library Cataloguing in Publication Data

```
Smith, Trevor, 1934-
Emotional health.
1. Mental hygiene
I. Title
613   RA790
```

WARNING

The contents of this volume are for general interest only and individual persons should always consult their medical adviser about a particular problem or before stopping or changing an existing treatment.

Insight Editions

WORTHING. Sussex
ISBN 0.946670.09.9

Printed and bound in Great Britain by
Biddles Ltd, Guildford and King's Lynn

"There is no blemish but in the mind."

Twelfth Night

Contents

Preface

A General Note on the Practical Exercises recommended

The exercises described are aimed as a stimulus only to learning, experiment and change, not as an end in themselves. Don't hesitate to change or alter any of the exercises if you think you can write better ones. But be careful that your own are not just easy comfortable alternatives. The exercises aim to help develop movements into alternative ways of thinking, new insights and understanding.

No exercise or recommendation should be seen as fixed or absolute, a recipe which must be absolutely adhered to, or even a complete answer to a particular area of problem. They are meant much more as stepping stones to new awareness. Your own ideas and exercises should be encouraged, developed and expanded as they occur to you. Practise the relevant exercises daily and any particular set of exercises for at least one month. If there is a specific problem area, the minimum time for practice is likely to be longer and you may need several consecutive months of work before you achieve significant real change.

Use the principles of 'brain-storming' whenever you come up against a particularly difficult problem. Allow all ideas, feelings, associations and phantasies to come up and be expressed over a period of half an hour, then apply the most useful ones to the problem area. During this time, completely suspend judgement and reality assessment. Write down all ideas however fantastic, futuristic or unreal, not just the practical, reasonable ones. Don't be cynical or judgemental of what comes up. Every idea is a part of you. Afterwards look more closely at these ideas and innovations. At first throw nothing away and see what aspects or fragments stimulate a new approach, and new ideas that help resolve a problem area. You may need time to understand your language and your own semantics but don't underestimate your creative potential.

If the exercises seem helpful and relevant, work at them regularly. If they seem irrelevant to you, then create your own alternatives and work on these. Don't be afraid to throw out any exercise which seems wrong but do replace it by a better one.

WARNING

If you are a patient, or have a psychological condition of any kind, which is being treated, do not suddenly and independently change or modify an existing course of therapy without first informing or consulting your doctor.

Introduction

Never before in the history of man has there been a time of so much technical advance and social change as has occurred in the past two decades. For the first time real opportunities for personal development and expansion, together with sufficient time and leisure are a reality for everyone. Cut-price budget travel places global contacts within everyone's reach and the chances of challenging and enriching encounters are no longer a dream but a reality.

At more mundane practical everyday levels, the super- and hyper-markets have greatly eased the burden of shopping and helped peg prices. Advances in labour-saving electronics, gadgets and easy-care fabrics have also gained precious time from otherwise dull, non-creative routines and time-absorbing chores – time which can now be used for more creative leisure and cultural pursuits as well as for contacts with others.

Adult and further education courses like the Open University give opportunities for study, development, dialogue and knowledge at every age and level, creating exciting new possibilities for personal development, previously unthinkable. With every time-saving technical advance literally at our fingertips, from the programmed dishwasher to the self-timing oven – there is now greater than ever opportunity for learning, listening and expanding whatever the aim, interest and time available.

In some ways, the arrival of the 80's has made Orwell's "1984" look tame by comparison and finally man seems at last to be in an enviable position where, at the touch of a button, the world is indeed his oyster.

Yet, at the same time as so much increased personal opportunity and time-availability for creative pursuits – time, perhaps not always from choice, never has there been so much personal pressure on the individual. There are demands to be different, pressures to change – habits, life-style, patterns and situations. The change is often from the known and the familiar to confirm the expectations and statistics of the politician, economist and planner. Man is told to conform and that he or she must 'fit in' with changes. With minimal consultation he or she is *told* how to be, rather than *consulted*, but how the individual actually is, feels and fears, is only rarely learned from first-hand experience.

Having moulded himself over the years into a conforming, trouble-avoiding peg, with a

4

familiar and comfortable way of working, he or she is told to re-adapt, to apply new techniques, new skills, but rarely with adequate time, explanation or preparation for them. We must suddenly conform to new aims and goals, modernise, be more mobile and flexible. All of this creates a restless reaction and counter-reactions, a division. Faced with galloping technical advances, there is less time for appraisal of the real individual, especially the psychological needs, adjustment-time and underlying fears. Each time these are ignored, there is panic or mistrust, sometimes psychological chaos, manifested externally as strikes and violence, lack of co-operation, diffidence or dis-ease, often illness in some form. Progress in modernisation tends increasingly to go ahead at a cost to the individual with the result that there is an alarming increase of both worker-sickness and community psychological ill-health.

These external pressures and changes are reflected in social disturbance and delinquency. This is now so generalised that no church door can safely remain unlocked outside service times, even in rural, traditionally 'safe' areas where house and car always remained open. There are few exceptions to the widespread expressions of violence and delinquency, commonplace in some form at every level of society. Crime is now so widespread that no major airport, railway station or store of repute is any longer a place of safety. At each moment it may become a target for a group or individual,

5

wanting to make a political point or to draw attention to its vulnerability.

The problem is not just a social one. Violence is also common at a personal level, usually suppressed, but direct open aggression is increasingly emerging as violence on the motorway and sports field and in the deprived community areas. In the main however, most violence ends up directed at the self and accounts for the disturbing increase in emotional illness, depression and suicide seen at every age. At least one patient in three now comes to the doctor with a problem that is directly psychological. The true figures are probably higher, as marriage and family are in such a state of confusion or disarray that one marriage in three ends in the divorce court within four years, and the 'norm' rather than the exception is for each classroom to contain at least one child from a broken marriage. It is no suprise that fewer people marry or want children, as the marriage commitment is increasingly seen as a 'high risk' involvement. There are few families in the UK without one adult child divorced by the age of thirty, and in the U.S.A. the figures are considerably higher. The breakdown of communication and meaningful dialogue, mainly as a direct result of television and video-addiction plus generalised attitudes of acceptance and passivity, adds considerably to the vulnerability of our family structure.

As a direct outcome of such pressures and suppressions, the social-addictive habits – drugs, alcohol or smoking, are on the increase and the total amount of tranquillisers and anti-depressants consumed in the UK and Europe is now extremely high. The exact amount taken is not accurately known, but the present annual national health drug bill is over two thousand million pounds, and a high percentage of this vast sum is directly attributable to psychological illness and the amount of tranquillisers and sedatives prescribed. The annual weight consumed per person of synthetic drugs runs into kilos rather than grams and gives a very clear indication of the degree of addiction, dependency and need for external props present in our society.

A major root-cause of emotional illness is the too rapid advance of technical development. There is minimal concern for the individual, as personal communication and dialogue lags behind the technical innovations. A facility with words in a new generation of professional communicators has meant an increased use of jargon. The short-cut, the quick and the immediate, give an impression of depth, meaning and openness which in reality hides the opposite. Words are too often now only used for cosmetic function, to disguise and mislead, with minimal growth of ideas, communication, expression and depth. As a result, frustration, lack of confidence and dissatisfaction with the spoken word are inevitable. As techniques become increasingly sophisticated, the presentation more professional and 'slick', so too what placates and is profitable becomes the major motivating forces, almost totally displacing ideals, principles, depth and values.

As everything becomes 'packaged', smaller, more convenient and instant, so too does the quality of the ideas behind them. Increasingly we are living in a world that is not just competitive – where there is healthy stimulation to growth, but one increasingly commercial, superficial and impersonal. Promotion psychology is injected into the unsuspecting consumer by the media at a cost to quality, durability and caring. Being commercial and 'sales efficient' is acceptable as long as there is an honest intention to benefit the consumer and not *just* to profit by him or her. It is now generally accepted that quality, reliability and service are almost things of the past, and few expect anything purchased to last more than a year or two because of the built-in deterioration factors.

The convenience foods of the supermarkets and monopoly stores have an artificially prolonged shelf-life based on profit motivations rather than those of health, concern for individual nutrition and health. All of this makes for an impersonal approach to the person and their needs, lessening the sense of mattering and of him or her being valued. Increasingly man senses himself as isolated, a pawn within an enterprise, a numerical calculation within a sales-exercise, rather than a valued human individual.

A major cause of confusion, fear and doubt is the absence of comment within the family to films or videos of sex and violence. The damage is not only because of the film and its content, but the lack of reaction and dialogue gives the young suggestible child, impressionable adolescent or immature adult, the impression of approval. Lack of comment is unconsciously felt as acceptance and assent even if not overtly expressed as such. Television, magazines, comics, films, videos are the major outlets upon the young and impressionable, and the main area where more open comment and dialogue are most needed. These are highly profitable markets, particularly where violence is linked to success, prestige, wealth, limelight sex or escape. None of this however gives a caring public what it really wants for their family and children, but little is done, except in the extreme cases of hard pornography and juvenile sex magazines, wrongly seen as most damaging because they disturb public morals while most of the violence is condoned.

Television shows insidiously damaging films of violence nightly, giving them maximum exposure, only lightly disguised as detective or 'who-dunnits'. All of this occurs within a climate of passivity and suggestibility, especially within a fragmenting family at a time when discussion and comment are almost non-existent because of a generalised 'don't know' acceptance or 'others know best'. There is misplaced anxiety about being thought different, 'square' and not modern, or that such films must be all right because they are 'on television'.

It would be incorrect and short-sighted to point a finger of responsibility in any one direction and too simple to state that our present social and health problems are the product of the selfish few, eager to gain at any price. The films and materials referred to have global distribution, particularly in the magazine and video-electronics field. The problem is much more the failure of the family to discriminate, discuss and criticise, rather than the material circulated. Violence needs a lot more understanding and discussion to prevent unhealthy identification, especially by the young. Anger is human and acceptable, different from violence. Anger ought to be expressed more openly, when it is felt, rather than left to fester without being admitted or talked about. Suppression leads to violent reactions from suppressed feelings. Where anger or violence are stimulated, but not admitted, acknowleged or challenged, it can in some temperaments escalate into uncontrolled violence – hence the importance of discussion and dialogue whenever the occasion demands it.

Modernisation is inevitable but because it is about of people and not just 'things', it also leads to casualties. especially where change is not a planned progressive step but the outcome of crisis. In industry there are too many sudden, unprepared – for, changes, which inevitably lead to counter-reaction. The pruning of a work-force that is over-manned and top-heavy also means pain and suffering. Such anguish is inseparable from our present problems of increasing industrial violence. Industrial delinquency in the form of picketing, lock-outs and unofficial or 'wild-cat' strikes. These are likely to continue as long as changes are made which are expedient rather than planned and which fail to consider the human needs, problems and fears. Industrial delinquency and emotional illness are often the same phenomen, with different areas of expression, but having the same roots in malaise, insecurity, mistrust and fear.

Before there can be healthy modernisation and re-structuralisation of industry, there must also be a re-structuring, education and preparation of the people concerned, their feelings, ideas, attitudes and thinking. Changes in a work-field are also inevitably changes in people. Where goals are long-term expansion, with concepts of creative expansion in the work-field the individual worker can identify, adapt, and adjust in a healthy way. Every individual needs to be able to identify with the particular task or problem area with which he or she is involved. This gives a healthy personal identification and change is made acceptable by discussion and feed-back, as occurs naturally in Japan. But in many other parts of the world there is total failure of dialogue, explanation and sharing, with no attention paid to the human factors concerned, to psychological preparation and the need for discussion and dialogue. The determination to change without discussion and consultation is inevitably a recipe for social disaster.

All illness, malaise, lack and frustration, either at an individual level or a more collective one is the direct result of wrong thinking, producing incorrect distorted imagery. This impairs understanding and judgement limiting spontaneity, contact, relationships and health. Negative thinking is just one example of how energy-drives are blocked by fear, prejudgement, apprehension and uncertainty.

The first step, often the only one of real importance, is to bring about a fundamental change in personal attitudes, asumptions and thinking. The way we think, listen, conceptualise, perceive, understand, respond and interpret is inseparable from psychological maturity, experience and overall health. Man's channels of creative expression, including the psychological ones, have the potential to convey such energies into form, and tangible shape and with a natural capacity to repair and heal. Where they are negative, distorted and misdirected, particularly into other areas not designed for them, they also cause a considerable undermining of health and well-being.

The positive outcome of well-directed psychological and creative energy streams is seen daily in the busy surgery, as the numerous spontaneous remissions and 'cures' which defy conventional explanation. These are quite wrongly called 'exceptions', when this is not the case, and every physician has examples of seemingly interminable difficult cases suddenly healing and resolving. Simply and paradoxically perhaps, there develops a more creative outlook and attitude, a significant change of thinking, often unconscious, which leads to physical change and cure. This may occur as an outcome of chance, a word, contact, visit or moment of insight. But it also happens when no easily definable reason or obvious happening has occurred to account for the change.

As positive growth within a social or industrial situation is inevitably preceded by changed, more progressive attitudes, so too malaise and illness are also preceded by negative, limiting attitudes which sap and undermine vitality, resistance and energy. Health is the end-product of a combination of positive attitudes and thinking, whatever the genetic constitution, the external stresses and demands. Open thinking creates open and available vitality. Inharmonious thinking and imagery creates panic, alarm, tension and witholding which have a depressing effect upon vitality.

Illness occurs because energies are depleted, run-down by closed-in thinking and imagery especially by unquestioned negative conviction and certainty. Once a negative thought process is engendered, it can drag the individual down completely and further reinforce other spirals of doubt, lack of confidence, weakness and disease.

The vulnerable, suggestible, aspects of man are most exploited by the media using images of acceptance, status, success, sexuality and fear for commercial gain and political manipulation. Whatever the levels of maturity, we are all to some degree affected by suggestion and media-processing because the techniques are both subtle and sophisticated. Allied to brain-washing, they stimulate uncertainty, doubt and fear of changing social and psychological attitudes. Because of the sophistication used, suggestion can be difficult to combat, even in health, especially where uncertainty or lack of information already causes confusion.

A negative conviction and belief held with sufficient intensity can in time bring into reality its own image and bitter fruit, confirming what is most feared and dreaded. This is in direct contrast to positive harmonising, thoughts and imagery which can equally bring into tangible reality achievement, harmony and health. The direction of the process cannot be altered easily, once a course has been set, as the deeper creative drives do not differentiate direction or outcome. This is why a prolonged, negative preoccupation or suggestion can be just as evocative as positive thought and imagery.

In order for change at any level to be lasting and permanent, the thought processes themselves must also be positive, open and harmonious. Where change is the expression of political or marketing techniques and manipulation, these have no links with real changes at a significant level, which is why they are short-lasting. Sustained, positive, thinking leads to more lasting changes with enormous potential for health, achievement and happiness.

Chapter one

The Basic Approach

Giving to Combat Taking

Giving is sharing of the true self in an outward, or 'other' action. It is not the giving of concrete, physical externals, such as presents and gifts which may have little real depth, however impressive the package, words or presentation. Too often 'things' are given instead of personal commitment, real identification and caring. True giving is also the letting-go and sharing of self and feelings, whether negative or positive, gentle or strong, to give out, as well as to listen and receive. Authentic giving ultimately develops and builds, leading to growth, confidence and strength.

Exercises in Psychological Giving

1 Avoid routine giving of presents and 'things' to friends or family other than for festivals, special occasions and anniversaries.

2 Try to express more of your real authentic self, feelings, reactions, interests and anger. Say when you are angry and talk about it. Don't just act angry to avoid a situation you can't cope with, nor 'storm out', 'wipe the floor' or flatten the other, when you are under pressure.

3 Put yourself in the position of others and try to understand *their* feelings and needs. Try to *be* them and see how they see you, their fears and anxieties and what they most need of you.

If you feel that others are making unreasonable demands on you, or manipulate you in some way, try to see what is *beneath* their actions and what the real fears and needs are. Be identified with them, try to understand how they perceive you, but don't lose yourself in the process of understanding others.

4 See how you can give and respond more to the deeper needs of others and try to do this. Don't only respond to surface needs, especially avoid responding in a superficial, trivial and repetitive way.

5 See clearly where you yourself are being manipulating. Others will often tell you if you ask, but you may also have to listen more in order to hear.

6 In general listen much more and talk less.

7 Write your own exercise here.

Closeness and Contact to Combat Alienation and Phantasy Build-up

Closeness with others, meaningful contact, softens the hard shell of self-interest and self-orientation. It is the best way to combat psychological alienation and withdrawal, or over-emphasis on phantasy, a world of fear, conviction and certainty. When phantasy-imagery spills over into reality and reality perceptions, distorting the picture of the outside world, it can also change conscious awareness into anxiety-tension, fear, panic, feelings of unreality, especially where contact with others is uncertain, weak, or minimal.

Exercises to Promote Closeness and Contact

1 Try to see your own routines, patterns and 'safe' contact. See how you control others, keeping them at a distance and why.

2 Once this is clear, try now to move more into different areas with others, to lessen the familiar patterns.

3   Once you have achieved a new area and a new situation, try to relate in a new, more open way. Especially listen more and give out more of you – as you are – not as you think you *should* be or others want you to be.

4   Try to get clear what is the essential you, your essence, intentions, drives and aims and then see how you can best express them in a way which most authentically reflects you.

5   Always try to understand the needs of others, for closeness, contact and sharing; seeing how you can best respond.

6   Try to see how closeness and contact are an intrinsic part of giving.

7   Write your own exercise here.

Self-caring for Health.

Self-care differs from narcissism and narrow self-interest. It is an attitude of caring that is vital to healthy development as long as it does not lessen encounter, closeness and giving. Trying to avoid negatives, unknowns and challenges is to avoid life itself. It is vital to have a maximum of varied exposures and experiences throughout life for maturity, perspective and wisdom. Self-caring is allowing such contacts to occur, staying sensitive without isolation or narcissism. Self-caring allows you to say 'no' to a situation which feels 'wrong' or damaging. It allows for some degree of self-protection without guilt, which preserves and protects at the same time as giving.

Where viewpoints and feelings can be defended and protected, in a spontaneous way, others can also be defended in an act of love and caring.

Where there is no love or respect for self, there can be none for others. Caring embraces self-needs as well as the needs and feelings of others. It is never possible to feel at ease with others unless you are first at ease with yourself, within your psychological envelope. It is almost a generality now, that most men and women dislike or do not care sufficiently for their body-shape and self-image. It is a common focal-point for self-attack, personal onslaught and negative self-imagery. All women and men have some need for display as part of their instinctive nature. When there is failure to care sufficiently for the self there is loss of confidence and a damaged sense of esteem which becomes a barrier to personal comfort, communication and relationships.

Exercises in Self-caring

1 Self-care is being defensive, but not being defended. Look carefully at any areas of inhibition where you insufficiently defend yourself, not wanting to cause offence, or where there is reluctance to disagree.

2 Understand, and get quite clear what self-care is, how it differs from self-interest and narcissm. Spend time to understand it in depth and diminish misplaced guilt. See clearly that caring for self is inseparable from caring for others.

3 Look at any situation where you are letting others dominate, influence, or manipulate you. Write them down and try to see their origins, and how these may have affected you over the years.

4 See how you can change attitudes of self-neglect and self-denial, but don't be too intellectual or theoretical about it. Decide how you can be more positive, more you and less defended.

23

5   Try to be less predictable in your relationships with others. If you can't change yourself in a relationship, consider stepping back, in order to be less masochistic and self-defeating.

6   Write your own exercise here.

Self-confidence for Health

Self-confidence is self-acceptance, not insisting on physical or intellectual perfection, acknowledging strengths and weaknesses as part of your overall totality. This sort of confidence is basic to sensitivity and receptivity, supporting contact and dialogue with others. It differs from self-satisfaction which has too much pride in it for health. Confidence is easily lost or damaged by pressure, strains and trauma, as the individual feels increasingly weak and vulnerable. Loss of self-confidence leads to malaise and unhappiness and these are some of the first signs of emotional disturbance.

Remember that no one can take confidence away from you, however much pressure is applied; only fear, phantasy and distortion of understanding, limit or destroy it because feelings are not allowed their full expression. It is often the holding-in of spontaneity which damages confidence, not the pressures of others.

Exercises in Building Self-confidence

1 See clearly where you lack confidence, the areas, people or persons involved and where you have most difficulty.

2 Having seen the problem areas, now look more closely at opposite areas where you are more confident and with whom. Try to see the difference, especially the way you expect others to be critical and how this influences your spontaneity.

3 Note how you feel others look at and see you, where you feel they are most critical. These are areas of personal vulnerability, weak areas of your own making – which you can strengthen and change by being less self-critical and demanding from yourself.

4 Put yourself in the other person's position – how they see and relate to you. Now defend yourself against criticism, standing up for your opinions and attitudes,

5 If you feel that the criticisms of others are justifiable, this is likely to weaken you. If they are justified, then try positively to alter and change in the area concerned. If they are not justified, then see why you are affected by them and any associated self-defeating guilt attitudes.

6 Try to clarify how and where you can be more self-confident and work out a programme of action for yourself which reflects the individual you really are.

7 Write your own exercise here.

Non-judgemental Attitudes to Combat Bias and Certainty

Absolute certainty is never possible in any psychological situation, even a personal one. Where people are concerned, certainty can only be approximate, and absolute judgement of others means rigid attitudes of knowing based on phantasy rather than a reality as it is happening. A non-judgemental attitude is not one that abdicates from responsibility and caring, but it refrains from attaching immediate labels, judgements and certainties which undermine. Where others are concerned, it is particularly important to have a suspended judgement, allowing for individuality and to help counteract personal blind spots and prejudices. Everything that happens is a true statement in some way even if it is a repetition or seems a mis-representation, particularly where fear, anxiety and previous hurts have occurred.

Exercises in Non-judgemental Attitudes

These may be helpful when there is a tendency for precipitate, harsh conclusions, or to be over-hasty with a quick tongue, followed by regret. Where there is a problem of short-fuse, weak-controls, the following exercises may assist, provided they feel right and are appropriate for the individual concerned.

1 Recognise any specific danger situations, or 'particular' people where you have a tendency to 'rush in'. Try to get these clear, and any other factors such as time of day, season, before or after a meal, before a period, business meeting or deadline which increases this tendency.

2 Having pin-pointed the weak danger areas, think of a situation in the last few weeks where you have been either rigid, biased or judgemental. Try to understand why. If it relates to a particular person or situation, see if this has ever happened before in a similar way. If there are earlier origins, see why and when.

3 Try to understand more why you are still importing old attitudes into the present. Where the problem relates to a specific person with no links to the past (rare), see what it is about that person and the particular relationship which makes you rigid or vulnerable.

4 See yourself more as others see you. Try to understand them more, their feelings about you, how they feel and respond when you act with such certain knowing.

5 Try to see yourself as being in command, acting and talking calmly however provoking, difficult and demanding, you feel the other person to be. Visualise yourself as calm and strong.

6 Practise distancing and spacing yourself from the immediate, so that you are there – interested and involved, but less intensively, a little more distant, and more of the onlooker.

7 Having thought your attitudes through, become less intense in reality situations. Above all be gentle, not rough or harsh. Being gentle with yourself means also that you can treat others in a more tolerant way too.

8 Write your own exercise here.

Dreaming to Combat Superficial Thinking and to Mobilise Deeper Psychological Levels.

Dreams are the Rosetta Stone of the mind whereby the hieroglyphics of the unconscious are given a more coherent symbolic structure and meaning. Such symbols are the conscious expressions of the unconscious – often a primitive unconscious with concrete inflexible impulses, and omnipotent drives. There are no greys within the unconscious and attitudes taken are absolute and total. They are closely allied to artistic expressions, of art, drama, dance and music and express a depth and a totality in every given situation.

Dreams play an important balancing role in our lives in addition to preserving sleep. They allow the surfacing and de-fusing of un-conscious material as well as contact with our depths however briefly. A problem left or slept on, is often resolved on waking from an enlightening dream, with a flash of new perspective and insight. The nightmare is a breakthrough of overwhelming fear, panic or phantasy into consciousness and may reflect a drug or toxic state, a high temperature, febrile illness or a deeper problem of insecurity. In general dreams are positive and only when we cannot dream do problems arise more severely because of the absence of their protective function.

Dreams often give important clues to un-conscious personal dynamics and can be an aid to solving psychological difficulties – panic, fear or doubt which defy logical explanation. Because dreams are couched in primitive symbolism, they are free from the usual verbal manipulations, jargon, cliché and reassurance, dreams have an integrity and an advantage over more conscious thinking. They often give insight into the depths of the unconscious and in this way can maintain balance and health. When shared, talked and thought about within a relationship, they lead to a greater depth of understanding, insight and knowing.

Exercises in Dream-Recall and Dream-work

1 Write down any dreams as and when they occur.

2 Record and note any forgotten dreams which are suddenly recalled. Such re-covered dreams are especially important.

3 Don't attempt consciously to analyse your dreams. As likely as not you will form wrong associations in order to maintain a sense or meaning for them.

4   Try more to link and develop a particular thought or feeling triggered-off by a dream. See also why you would want to forget them and get beneath the conscious levels of emotions and feelings. In this way you can more easily avoid the limitations and pitfalls of words, ideas and logic which control and manipulate insight and understanding.

5   If you can't understand the meaning or make a link with a dream just forget it and leave it be. Its major function always is a thought link-pin, a stimulus to feeling, and the same unconscious drives will surface in a new way as a different dream when you may recognise or link it with any previously obscure associations.

6   When a dream sets off a new train of thought, or forgotten memory, then it has fulfilled its function, inter-relating the past with the present in a coherent way as well as preserving vital rest and sleep.

7   Remember each dream only surfaces briefly, to be forgotten. Its aim is amnesia and balance, not to help you to remember. Dreams are unconscious thought images which aim at a compromise pictorial solution of unresolved emotional areas which otherwise would cause tension, and disturb peace of mind.

8　Write your own dream exercise here.

Faith and Psychological Health

Althought in many ways inseparable, they are also very different aspects which reflect the individual. Both are key to understanding and helping self or others. Faith is belief and confidence in something other and greater than man alone, a conviction of a spiritual harmonising force – however it is conceived and notioned. It is also a belief in the non-tangible, non-logical, more intuitive, non-definable, non-intellectual aspects of man which has links with his totality and concepts of the universe.

Faith is not easy to talk, define or write about. It varies enormously with each individual and throughout life, with periods of absolute, conviction, to times of seeming total doubt and even despair. It is always a very private aspect, yet inseparable from psychological balance and health. Faith has great healing depths, more sensed than felt. It can be lost during times of depression. stress, or alienation, yet recovered again in a more balanced, less self-orientated, self-destructive frame of mind. Within everyone, there is an intuitive, usually unspoken awareness of inspirational-creative forces as a depth within, which gives form and a deeper meaning to life where otherwise, only confusion, instinct, incoherence, predominate. Faith is not about any established belief, religion, sect, God or even spiritual concept. It is more related to trust, an awareness of natural relationships, developments, shape, form and order in life and happenings. It can occur just as strongly with a conviction about a particular social or political order, ideal or cause. Faith only becomes a potential negative when it becomes altered by judgemental, puritanical or dogmatic concerns, too concrete and absolute or driven by pride, lessening its depth, sensitivity and contact with the inspirational sources. The creative-inspirational root of man is the ultimate source of all caring, sensitivity, insight and understanding, and faith is the strength which these deeper origins inspire.

The relevance of faith to psychological health is that it supports belief in something other and outside the immediate self, personal satisfactions, wishes and desires. Faith strengthens and harmonises with vital energy. It plays a part in organising creative drive into form, shape and order. Such creative expressions are the only ones that truly give confidence, satisfaction, ease, contact and expression, maintaining health and balance.

Exercises in the Awareness of Faith

1 To talk of exercises in faith seems almost to limit or diminish it in some way. But this is not the intention. The aim is to enhance awareness of its presence even at times of stress, when it seems absent or irrelevant.

2 If you have lost faith, it is probably lost in one formal setting only – probably a religious one, which no longer has meaning or relevance to you just now. Even if you have lost religious conviction, you have probably not totally lost faith, but fail to recognize it.

3 Try to separate yourself from past, earlier beliefs and situations. You can't do this entirely because to some extent the past is a part of you, but nevertheless make the attempt to separate yourself as you are today from the you as you were or have been.

4 Once you can establish yourself more in the present, you will feel more of a person again, able to function more clearly. See what you believe in. It may be the state, it may be nature, it may be a belief in nothing, or a strong conviction in something which you feel but cannot give words to.

5   Ignore the form and shape of your beliefs for
    the moment, because if you have lost faith,
    you may also be confused or depressed and
    your creative-inspirational drives have to
    channel their expressions through alter-
    native path-ways. Once you have found your
    beliefs, you will be in a better position to see
    if this is really and truly you, how you see
    things now. Give yourself lots of time for
    these exercises.

6   Write down here your own exercise in the
    awareness of faith.

Being Centred for Psychological Health and Balance

All of us draw strengths, balance and harmony from at least four major areas, which are fundamental to security and health. Any one of these may take over the other, the experience and perception of the outer world, altering also the responses and attitudes to others.

The four major energy areas are:

1 The psychological needs and their expression. In isolation they may lead to excesses of emotional lability, the feelings too fluid or intense in expression and degree.

2 The inspirational-creative needs and expressions. These may be too ideal, self-righteous or puritanical, when in excess, or ethereal, remote and not-of-this-world, at the other extreme.

3 Physical needs and their expressions. In isolation they can lead to shallowness, lack of depth and over-emphasis on the physical and the immediate at a cost to sensitivity and maturity.

4 Logical thinking and intellectual functioning. If excessive they lead to the boffin or theorist, over-intellectual, con-

trolled, stiff and narrow. Feelings and emotional insights are limited by excessive intellectualisation.

It is important that each energy area is in balance with the others and that neither is over-whelming and excessive, nor absent and suppressed for health.

1 We need to be in touch with feelings and emotions but not too emotional or, driven and over-influenced by the senses, ideas and phantasy at the expense of discernment, reasoning and reality, especially for the needs and feelings of others.

2 It is important to be in touch with the inspirational self but not to go 'overboard' over religion at a cost to real charity, sensitive caring, giving and loving.

3 It is also important to be in contact with physical energies, the body-self, and to enjoy them, but at the same time, not to be excessively external and only physically orientated to the detriment of intuition.

4 It is important to stay clear-thinking, logical, coherent and rational but not too much either. Being intellectual, or brilliant with a flow of words and reasons, tends to explain away rather than to clarify, in an over-tangible, too well defined way.

Being centred implies being in touch with all four energy areas, yet not letting any one overwhelm, dominate or pressurise the other, however much one particular area may have been given emphasis and weight in the past.

Exercises in Staying Centred

1 Sit quietly, listen and sense the four major energy areas at work within you. The physical will quickly make itself known as it seeks to envelop you, seeking comfort or stimulation by restlessness. Cultivate an awareness of breathing or heartbeat.

2 Psychological associations often surface as feelings about the past, the now and the future. They too should not be allowed to over-influence other areas, although their sensitivity and awareness is very important.

3 The intellectual processes are the flow of thoughts and ideas which constantly emerge into your mind. Thoughts should be allowed to emerge, but not to dominate overall sensitivity, thinking-intuition, or awareness of a particular relationship or experience.

4   The inspirational-creative is felt when other
    areas are quiet. Listen for its deeper notes
    and tones, especially listening for its drive
    and direction as the new and creative. It
    does this constantly, if you will allow it
    enough space, expression and opportunity.

5   When out of balance practise this listening
    and awareness in depth daily, until each
    energy stream is clearly sensed, felt and
    known about.

6   Write your own exercise here.

Being Centred for Self-Expression

The psychologically-centred person is in emotional balance, not thrown off course by emotional demands, overwhelming reactions or responses to them. The centred person is flexible, able to acknowledge and accept feelings and responses without being unduly upset and overwhelmed, at risk or damaged by them. Fear, tension and anxiety are all compromises on internal reality. When psychologically in a more central solid position, doubt, anger, fear can come up and be acceptable and expressed according to the situation. At the same time such feelings can also be tested-out against life's realities – meaning others and the experience of them, without feeling threatened in the process. Both are important. It is just as important to know that we will not overwhelm as be overwhelmed. When centred, we are in the best psychological position to know this.

When psychological foundations are optimistic, there is greater sensitivity to human need and vulnerability, which need not imply however, fragility, collapse, loss of confidence, strength or composure.

Not fearing being overwhelmed, means being able to respond with spontaneous feelings without harmful denial or suppression. Creative ideas, responses, joy, are all possible as long as there is no deviation from a central overall position of psychological harmony. Although it is fundamental for everyone to stay centred, it does not always happen automatically. Because of stress, external demands and pressures as well as internal ones, staying in balance is a position which is precarious at time and needs insight and awareness to maintain it.

Exercises in Staying Centred for Greater Self-Expression

1 Try to see your weak areas, patterns of feelings, especially familiar ones, where there are repetitive reactions – anger, rivalry, jealousy, criticism, or passivity and acceptance. These may drive you off-course and leave you upset, drained, depressed or depleted.

2 Map these out carefully to see how and when they occur. Ask a close friend, if you can't see clearly when they happen. But if possible rely as much as you can on your own objective, intuitive senses.

3　Once the main areas are clear, you may feel that they are too conscious. But you must begin somewhere, and the fact that you are aware of them does not lessen their significance.

4　Having recognized and clarified the areas, when next they occur, try quite consciously not to let yourself be pulled into the same patterns. If it involves one particular person, then you are probably also contributing to the situation and colluding. If the problem is more generalised, there may also be some manipulation and distortion of your making. Try to see all of these points, and especially your own role, as clearly as possible.

5　If you can see any roots or origins as to the reason for such patterns of involvement – well and good. If you can't see the causes clearly, then don't try to intellectually analyse the situation, because this will only lead you further away from insight developing.

6　More important is that when a similar situation next occurs, that you are aware of it, and that you try to lessen your own reactions and their intensity. Do this especially at the time, becoming a little less involved, less intense, more at ease, natural and relaxed without always judging or expecting a negative response from others.

7 Write your own exercise here for staying centred.

Staying Centred for Greater Self-awareness

The emphasis here is on staying more consistently in touch with ideas and feelings at the time they emerge, especially intuitive, creative-inspirational ones. In this way, the pressures of others, their demands and manipulations as well as their giving, needs and caring can be kept in perspective. With increased sensitivity to self-awareness, there is greater understanding of the inspirational self as an outward, *other* looking depth and expression of self.

Exercises to Help Develop Self-Awareness

1 Self-awareness is awareness of you – as you are now – your aims, feelings, actions and goals, how you are changing, learning, growing and evolving *this* moment – not in the past nor the future.

2 It is based on giving more time, emphasis and listening to the situations, feelings and problems which arise. Repetitive patterns of behaviour and response hide and suppress

the real, more vulnerable, evolving you, because it seems frightening and unfamiliar and the process of change is resisted.

3 Once patterns have been perceived, they should not be suppressed or 'cast out', but rather tolerated and watched – as if from a distance. In this way you can slowly withdraw yourself from them, become softer, less harsh, and definite, more humorous about the process of change, your psychological defences and habitual attitudes. Suppression is never positive, even of the apparently negative and unhelpful. The best action always is friendly tolerance, observation and awareness. In this way you can also be more tolerant and aware of others.

4 Write your own exercise here.

Staying Centred for More Balanced Situation-Responses

When centred, we are more in touch with the true self, more aware of drives and forces within, which are constantly striving for exit and expression. This gives greater awareness, perception and depth so that each new experience and 'meeting' can be experienced with more sensitive intuition and a spontaneous creative response. When the situation is stress-laden, or emotional, being centred allows for more balanced overall responses, rather than pattern-behaviour based on assumption, past experience, previous hurt and damage. Situation-appraisal means being able to respond appropriately in terms of the total self at the time and not being dominated by either past or future fears.

Exercises in Sensitivity to Situation-Response

1   Treat every personal encouter on its merits, as it happens, acting spontaneously and openly. Where a situation evokes anger, flight, avoidance or withdrawal, provided

that it is appropriate and not part of a repetitive pattern, you should express these feelings as they occur, at the time.

2 If you are able to be consistently relaxed, flexible and different with each situation – well and good. If you are on guard, seeing danger all the time or are excessively gushing and over-familiar, then you are probably not centred and your situation-response is likely to be inappropriate or limited. This is an important loss to you of an authentic encounter and contact. It should be corrected as soon as possible by carefully analysing (understanding) each situation and the patterns triggered-off by it.

3 Try to be more balanced within each new situation as it occurs. Practise listening, avoiding pre-judgement. Especially be more spontaneously you in each situation, as it occurs. Each contact is different in some way and so should you be. Life and you constantly evolve, develop and make movement into new perceptions, new understanding and new growth.

4 Write your own exercise here.

Staying Centred for Balanced Perception

Where there is an overall perception of what is seen, felt and observed, not limited or distorted by assumption-patterns, there can be a deeper realisation of each situation and contact. When each encounter is clearly expressed and more other-orientated, this helps giving to be less defensive and to be less self-orientated. As more individuality is allowed expression, spontaneity and decision-making can also emerge with greater originality and flexibility. In this way, what is seen and felt, confirms not only what is experienced, but also the more intuitive, intangible aspects.

Exercises in Perception

1 Perception means how you look, see, understand and respond. It reflects and differentiates who you are now from how you were before, have grown, matured and changed. Try to see clearly how your perceptions have evolved and how the way you 'see' a situation now has changed over the years.

2 As we mature, so too the details, breadths, subtleties, non-verbals and intangibles of a relationship and situation become clearer. Try to see in what way and to what depth you experience each different relationship.

3 Clarify which of your contacts have a depth and a flexibility to them and others which are narrower, flatter, more limited or stagnant. Try to see why this is and how you can deepen or improve them.

4 Listen more and generally be less cautious. See the roles you play in keeping relationships superficial and why. Try to let these develop and deepen. Where there seems to be a danger or a threat, see why and upon what reality this is based.

5 Try to perceive, listen and be more intuitive in your difficult relationships. Take the other person's 'side' and see where you agree or disagree. Imagine yourself as them – listening to you. Try to see how they see, respond and understand you, the impressions, openness and 'vibes' you generate. See how the difficulties you create are part of the overall impression you give out and the reactions you bring about.

6 Write your own exercise here.

Flexibility in Responding to Others

The ability to trust – ultimately oneself as much as another, leads to more open expression, less restriction and control, without needing to have the answer, immediately, or to be right all the time.

More important than always having solutions, is willingness to learn, listen, share and be more open, ready to look at alternatives. Knowing, and having to be right to prove a point, to confirm an established position or avoid change, usually reflect weakness and fear rather than strength.

Trusting others without insistence on guarantees and certainties implies a maturity and a confidence. Everything expressed has a truth and an accuracy to it, however poetic this seems. Each understanding, thread and theme has an element of life, truth and expression, however unrecognized or obscure at the time.

Exercises in Flexibility

1 These are important because without flexibility of mind, there is not flexibility of attitudes and this can cause stubborn

moodiness. It should not be confused with weakness or passivity, which are different. Flexibility is willingness to consider change and to work with alternatives. It allows new contacts, ideas or experience to stimulate and perhaps modify an established perception or viewpoint, so that there is a greater choice of expression available and a more meaningful richness of experience. It opens up new concepts and ideas, other ways of looking and responding.

2 Where there is inflexibility of attitude, there is also rigidity and stasis of mind. Opposition to change and growth often comes from reluctance and fear of not being able to cope or manage new demands.

3 Look at the areas where you are most rigid. In order to do this you will have to look where you feel most certain and definite, most sure. It is often felt as something that is so known as to make discussion superfluous. These rigid attitudes and thought structures are also areas of pride and you may need to reconsider where this is most marked.

4 You will probably not actually see yourself as rigid, but look at the areas where you are firm and certain. You will probably find yourself not wanting to listen or consider the opposite viewpoint. Try to understand your reasons for this and any challenge it poses. Look more closely at the major

aspects of your personality, style and especially your psychological assertions. Reconsider these for rigidity or lack of flexibility.

5   Look at the situations where you are most definite and certain. Consider these as possible areas of weakness and vulnerability, bolstered up by rigidity. Try to understand and to soften them as they happen. Allow other viewpoints more time for listening, and discussing as they occur, rather than later and in retrospect.

6   Write down your own exercise here.

Feelings – A General Statement

Feelings are what we consciously experience of the inner unconscious emotional affective self. They are the most available peripheral sensations we have of our inner psychological world. Because they mirror and reflect a phantasy world, often without reference to reality, they can also misrepresent, convey faulty impresssions and a wrong understanding of reality. Like reflected shadows from an inner flame, they lead us to believe that their flickering imagery is reality rather than a response to inner perceptions, with no direct relationship to the world as it is happening.

Positive Feelings and Ambivalence

Positive feelings are important as a reassuring part of our totality and for the sense of completeness and comfort they bring. They are however always inseparable from other, ambivalent impulses, to withdraw, defend, take flight, or attack as well as the more trusting ones. Only the admission, acceptance, and recognition of intrinsic ambivalence can make us fully human and help to lessen omnipotent judgements, stress, and certitude. Positive feelings may mean warmth, love and trust, but they can also be based on fear. The truly positive must inevitably contain within its depths some element of the negative for completeness, to give it a more poignant meaning, which is why being human and involved can also be such a painful experience.

Negative Feelings

These are the inseparable doubts and opposites to trust, love and closeness. They are sometimes uncontrolled or excessive where there has been past damage or when the need for caring is lost sight of. Anger and rage may be a response to provocation, or rejection, the threat of loss, causing feelings of vulnerability. In this way closeness and caring may also become associated with rejection, leading to reactions of defence, even hostility, which seems paradoxical at the time.

Neurosis

Neurosis is a state of psychological imbalance when unresolved, isolated parts of the self flood over into perception, thinking and judgement, causing reactional excesses. There is both denial and an intensity within the intrinsic love-hate ambivalence which becomes attached to every relationship. Phantasy-imagery, often infantile in origin, invades and distorts reality experience, causing tension and emotional reaction. Contact with others is consistently disturbed or undermined as powerful feelings spill-over, to produce replicas or vignettes of past hurts in an effort to re-live as well as to control them. The repetition tendency is often mistaken for other things, but it almost inevitably leads to greater hurt and to further re-confirmation of rejection and failure, being misunderstood or unloved.

In health, there is an invisible boundary which keep conscious and unconscious imagery apart from reality so that meeting, contact and experience are not excessively distorted, or lost to reality. Some trauma and hurt are an inevitable part of every growing up experience, and should not be suppressed or denied. Old hurts need both tolerance and expression to soften them, so that their bound energy can play a more positive role in the present. In this way feelings of deprivation and resentment which would otherwise undermine growth and stunt creative expression can merge into an overall totality, be less isolated and also be less damaging.

Motivation, Aims and Goals to Combat Neurosis

Where motivations are primarily inner directed towards self-interest and self-gain, the protective and the immediate, rather than giving-out, sharing or closeness, this undermines the fullest development of personality. The experience of unselfish giving leads to enriching growth and expansion because it identifies with the person or situation given to.

Health is ultimately the ability to experience and respond to change with sensitivity and to allow a re-experiencing of other layers of closely-related experience to be awakened by the contact or situation. As the essential self is gradually less defended, more open, each experience of others leads to greater depth and perception, to more understanding and growth.

Exercises in Healthy Motivation

1   For part of each day, either at work or in the family, avoid contacts and situations which are largely motivated by self-interest, reassurance, or comfort.

2 Aim to be and to act, without gaining motive, to be you now, to experience, respond and give-out spontaneously with feeling, ideas, thoughts and reactions.

3 Do this in situations which you know and recognize as safe or familiar. Try to understand the needs and feelings of others more. Then see why their needs are there and give at this level rather than at a more superficial self-interested one.

4 Next heighten awareness in other relationships with less obvious patterns. Try to avoid self-reassurance and comfort at a cost to the quality of closeness, of communication and each relationship or encounter.

5 Write your own exercise here.

Why Neurosis Undermines and Distorts

Neurosis is always based on an imaginative, phantasy-assumption conception of the present rather than any actuality of the situation. It may follow an actual hurt or trauma which serves to concretise and reinforce its patterns, especially fear, rage and anxiety. It is always an over-reaction in the present with a re-creation of some aspect of an actual or phantasy-past.This is clung to for reasons of familiarity and reassurance, in the mistaken belief that in this way it is possible to control an evolving present. Neurosis undermines because it distorts reality into a framework from the past. Where life is an emergence, a chain of new unfoldings rather than an extension or repetition of the past, it is less dominated by neurotic assumption and former patterns.

Neurosis distorts because of its insistence on an endless re-play of old scenes, the constant attempts to bring about a re-staging of earlier dramas only superficially changed by a new casting in the present. Neurosis may seek to reassure, but above all, it tries to re-prove old assumptions and beliefs by preserving old patterns and re-enacting them within the new. The constant attempt to re-interpret and to slant the emerging now, limits creativity, drive, the ability to perceive and to respond spontaneously.

Neurosis refuses to see the world of the present as it is now. Much of what is seen, felt and perceived is a shadow of reality because of the constant importation of old imagery. The distortions are never new, they have happened many times before in an attempt to retain the same basic assumptions and patterns. The constant re-affirming of neurotic assumption reinforces itself because it is negative and narcissistic. Creative-inspirational drives tend to become blocked or confined to narrow channels of outlet and expression which limit their variation of expression and form. All of this creates a faulty, inaccurate viewpoint in understanding the world, based on a past that is assumption-loaded because of immature emotions. Trust, closeness, giving and love are all influenced by excessive phantasy, often infantile, and life's essentials – spontaneity and vitality – are kept under lock and key. This blockage to confidence and giving confirms and perpetuates the neurotic assumptions and beliefs.

The Many Heads of Neurosis

Neurosis can present itself in many different bewildering ways – which seem reasonable at the time – and only later, in retrospect, is their distortion and unreality apparent. Attitudes appear sound and plausible, yet their repetition within a wide range of different areas and contacts draws attention to the emotional nature of the opinions held and their lack of objectivity.

Fear, exhaustion, anxiety, insecurity, doubt, loneliness, dissatisfaction, envy, jealousy, excessive competition, loss of confidence, and chronic failure-syndromes are just some of the symptoms and outlets of neurosis. There may be more physical manifestations, such as clumsiness, accident-proneness, pain, weakness, travel-sickness, travel-phobia, insomnia, nausea, dis-ease and agitation when in contact with others and commonly associated with a repetitive, obsessional pattern of behaviour.

Where the problem is deeper and more severe, then distorted beliefs with inappropriate behaviour can occur. Suspicion, mistrust, depression, irritability or excessive anger with loss of control may occur. Constant negative attitudes of self-denial, self-denigration, self-hate may be experienced as a criticism or persecution from others and add further to the basic problems.

Physical symptoms are particularly common, especially involving muscles and tendons with tics or spasm from the excessive nervous energy and excitability. Pain from spasm and paralysis, from loss of vitality and energy flow also occur. Other common complaints are fainting, collapse, circulatory disturbances such as sweating, blushing, palpitations, backache, headache, diarrhoea, indigestion, loss of sexual interest and menstrual problems. All are part of the underlying emotional disturbance putting pressure on normal physiological functioning. A preoccupation with body-image is frequent in either obesity or anorexia. There may also be a whole variety of long-standing 'nervous' symptoms such as cough, diarrhoea, loss of voice, urinary frequency, acidity, heart-burn or spasm in any part of the body which defy both diagnosis and satisfactory treatment.

Many such symptoms are perpetuated by long, drawn-out hospital investigations or treatment with little information given, usually emphasising the external, the physical and the body, rather than any internal or psychological cause. Much of the delay and uncertainty is because the symptoms and causes are obscure and difficult to diagnose, closely mimicking other conditions. Because neurosis is such a good imitator and identifies very closely with a physical illness it can obscure the *true* cause, delaying diagnosis and appropriate treatment for months or even years.

Other Neurotic Attitudes, their Importance and Resolution

1 Alienation

Being cut off from others also means being cut off from self, leading to psychological alienation, weakness, impoverishment of experience and relationships. This internal separation also leads to loneliness, isolation and depression. Alienation may have a straightforward physical cause like deafness – for example following mumps. Visual and speech impediment can also interfere with the vital flow of sensory information. Arthritis may be another isolating factor. Environmental isolation has become increasingly common, with the modern impersonal style of life in high-rise flats or just the general anonymity of urban living. It is particularly common in the elderly where a retirement move separates from the familiar, or when changing to a new area, either rural or urban where new contacts may be difficult to make. A retirement lump sum, or windfall late in life, leading to a larger, more comfortable house, a more clement area, can also exact a considerable toll in terms of friendship and contact in the new environment which may never be fully resolved. The long-awaited move can cause severe loneliness and loss of friendships, rather than a rewarding experience of joy, companionship, and contact.

Alienation is one of the most serious of present day problems. The commonest causes are psychological and include depression, anxiety, lack of confidence, agoraphobia or mental illness. Such problems often pass unrecognized in the immediate environment because it is easier to see them at a distance rather than close to home. They are rarely helped by formal religion or the social agencies, unless there is a personal contact, as loss of faith is commonly present. A 'masked' depression is easily misinterpreted as remoteness, when what is really needed is a much more caring closeness and contact with others. Giving may not be easy when there is depression and loneliness, the feeling of being too old or not valued. But giving-out and caring for others is essential to heal the inner psychological splits which intensify alienation, whatever the physical and environmental factors present.

Exercises to Reduce Alienation and Isolation

1 Stop feeling sorry for yourself, blaming others for your difficulties. Every psychological problem is self-generated to some extent and you cannot expect others to come first to you. You must go out to others more.

It is the lack, or reluctance to go out, to give to others which ultimately causes the feeling of alienation and failure.

2 Define clearly your daily patterns, the places, time of day, when and where you see others. Don't stay at home alone, feeling sorry for yourself. Consider changing both time-table and patterns in order to be more flexible and available for others.

3 Make more effort to talk and give out to others. Find out what you can do in the community, where there is most need. Consider voluntary work of some kind through your local church, hospital or a charity shop. Try to be more active and generous with your time, practical advice and energy where the need is greatest.

4 If you dislike the above suggestions, and the ideas seem totally foreign or unwelcome, nevertheless try them or something similar, at least for a few weeks.

5 Make sure that you yourself are not turning a blind eye to the needs of others, the depression or alienation of other people, feeling sorry for yourself, but withdrawn and not helping in their areas of most need.

6 Be more of a friend. Don't be a bore by talking about *your* problems and needs. See how you can understand and help them

more and what practical steps or advice you can give.

7 If you have a physical limitation, like arthritis or deafness, do something positive about it – perhaps a new hearing aid, or an alternative approach, trying to become more mobile. If you are totally immobilised or house-bound from a physical cause, still try to give out more and be more interested in the contacts you have. Do something for *others* in need. Do this from your own room if necessary, but make contacts and have a more positive aim which involves greater giving out. Caring and concern for others is fulfilling as well as therapeutic, even for severe problems which handicap and confine. If you are confined physically, don't be confined psychologically and don't allow yourself to be defeated by it.

8 Write your own exercise here.

2 Putting Off And Delaying

When based on fear or doubt, delaying is part of avoidance with everything left to the last moment – paying a bill, opening or answering a letter, making a social contact or commitment. Every aspect of living and communicating is delayed – in the hope that it will go away, from fear of failure, rejection or a sense of inadequacy. Life is lived in a frenzy of anticipated disaster and a threatening future, rather than an evolving present. Delays signify attempts to control and maintain psychological sameness, to preserve the *status quo*, the known familiar. The result is always weakness of personal confidence because experience and trust can only be developed by experiencing and responding to a challenge as it occurs and not by delaying to the last possible moment.

The attempt is to delay life itself as everything is made into a threat. There can be no guarantees in personal contacts and involvement, and what is denied now has inevitable psychological implications later. Like all neurotic defences, only the individual perpetuates them, and always at a considerable cost to personal growth and security.

Because there can be no absolute certainties of the unfolding moment, reality as it happens, the present is held to ransom by delaying tactics made up of past imagery and feared phantasy. Constant delays until the last moment means that the experience of the now is limited and kept minimal because it is rushed or defensive. Time is not allowed for adequate thinking, awareness, or contact, so that each experience is also a weak one. Relying on phantasy-expectation rather than reality-experience, reinforces neurotic anticipation and fears but offers little to the processes of change, insight, or growth.

Exercises in Combating Putting-off and Delaying.

1   Make a careful note of everything you are delaying or putting-off, especially in areas where you repeatedly act in this way.

2   Try to understand your conscious reasons for delaying and how it first started. See if you procrastinate more in one area than another. Try to clarify if this is from fear and insecurity or from a more generalised negative expectation about life.

3   You may find that you delay in some areas of life where you would like more time rather than less. Start at least to give yourself more time in any important areas

which are being neglected. Gain time by cutting-down on analysing, anticipating, fearing and predicting.

4 Practise in areas where you most frequently delay by responding more spontaneously – to an invitation or a more feared situation. Test-out and confirm that phantasy-expectations are never as bad as reality. Do this frequently until you gain more confidence.

5 Once you have worked-out and gained experience and confidence in the major delaying areas, begin the same work in less obvious areas. Understand their symbolic meaning where possible, why you are distorting and delaying even if knowing 'why' takes a little longer.

6 Write your own exercise here.

3 Fear

Fear feeds on distortion which alters judgement and creates misunderstanding, so that phantasy-perception predominates over reality. Fears distort and create nightmare situations from trivial happenings, overwhelming the most mundane happenings by imposing their phantasy-imagery on them, taking over, distorting, and undermining reality.

When fears predominate, they exclude the present by constantly translating each meeting and encounter into a threat. Life and reality is changed by fear into a – 'high-risk' experience of danger, panic and terror. Fear may paralyse drive and internal impulses to act spontaneously and to be. They can also reflect pressures to be more of a person and to break out of a depressing, stagnant psychological situation.

General Exercises to Lessen Fear

(For more specific examples see the relevant chapter.)

1   In a situation where you feel afraid or fearful become more low-key and relaxed. There is usually no reality to the threats and dangers, they are self-imposed and self-generated. A real danger threat situation needs different treatment, action to protect yourself and to alter it. Diffentiate anxiety-fear situations from those where there is an active risk or danger and clarify the difference between them. See how you respond in a real tangible crisis, rather than a phantasy one.

2   Once you clearly see that fear comes from within, is generated by you, begin to see how the psychological threats are created and generated by yourself. Try to see the gains and motivation of self-generated fear, however illogical and unreal this seems just now.

3   Try to experience and explore each feared situation. You need to do this in order to correct distorted assumptions concerning the situation and the reasons for your self-imposed weakness and vulnerability. You are probably over-exaggerating supposed 'dangers' at the same time as underplaying

your own strengths to perpetuate a situation of 'no change'. It is however a 'no-change' to health, happiness and growth.

4 Increase self-exposure daily to others until you learn that you are not so vulnerable as your neurosis would portray you to be.

5 Write down your own exercise here.

4 Spectator Attitudes

A typical peripheral, on-looker attitude prevails, largely uninvolved and on the side-line. Such attitudes are often critical and intellectual as well as distant, sometimes cruel or cutting because they lack the softening of closeness, understanding and involvement. Spectator distancing weakens because as it cuts off a supposed threat or demand it also separates from inner awareness. Spectator-logic limits closeness and contact to safe situations where feeling-involvement is minimal.

Living in a world with minimal emotional or sharing contact leads to impaired psychological balance and incorrect understanding so that reality becomes only interpreted in terms of self-interest and self-protection. With few real involvements and close relationships, there is little to correct observer-attitudes. The spectator skates through life on thin ice but is rarely in contact closely with others. It is enough to be present, counted but not involved. The spontaneous reactions of joy and over-whelming feeling are not permitted except in 'safe' familiar situations – in case there is loss of control. Denial of psychological reality deprives the inspirational self of most personal creative outlets so that life becomes contracted or contrived. Being on the touchline of life, the spectator is out of contact also with his or her intuitive self which gives a more balanced appraisal, a less harsh judgement and perception of others. The constant withdrawal into states of observation or comment-at-distance leads to personality weakness, loss of experience, and constricted creative drive. The onlooker sees life as a *fait accompli*, as an act or fact already passed and played. In this way – there is no reason to look, feel or listen – the whole of life is a past event. But also the spectator is an onlooker on life as well as within himself.

Exercises to limit Spectator-mind Attitudes

1 Try to let other people be more themselves. Don't prejudge them before they have made their contributions or contact – however large or trivial.

2 See where you are most spectator-orientated and begin to change there. Allow yourself to experience others more as they are, for better or worse – but always as they are. Don't make assumptions about them, unless from contact or reality experience.

3 Try to see why you are afraid and where you are trying to control. Try, even in a small way, to make more real contact with others,

to let them get closer to you by being more genuinely interested.

4   Try to develop greater awareness of where and how you are remote and with whom. Start to loosen-up in these areas by giving-out more, witholding comment and judgement.

5   Treat others whom you group or pigeon-hole, as people and not as clichés or members of a structure which you have formed in your mind.

6   When the problem centres around a particular person, a rivalry situation with a colleague or older, parental-authority figure, try to lessen convictions and assumptions, whatever the links with the past. See others as people and show them the person you are so that their assumptions may also be corrected and balanced.

7   Write your own exercise here.

5 Intellectualisation

The intellectual defence against closeness, feeling and involvement is one of the most difficult a physician or counsellor has to deal with and rivals mental illness in its rigidity, complexity and apparent reasonableness. Such convictions are difficult and prolonged because they seem so persuasive, based on reason and logic. But ultimately they alienate, distance, and explain away rather than truly reflect an actuality of the now. The intellectual defence seeks to avoid by a flood of reasons, logic and explanation to control any threat of loss of control in areas they feel to be vulnerable.

Intellectual reasoning is later in development than the intuitive-sensitive aspect of the mind and lies largely superficial to it. The more vulnerable psychological self, with sensitive feelings, needs, impulses and fears is in contrast to the colder, factual, intellectual certainty of observable proof, measurable information, and logic. Such logical and controlled expressions can undermine intuitive truth and are the antithesis to spontaneity of self-expression, and creative problem-solving.

Everything can be disputed or brought to nothing by skilful intellectual argument and persuasion, as is well-known in the commercial and political world. The basic, real, human feelings in any situation are the only ones which matter or are ultimately meaningful. An intuitive sense is key to meaningful dialogue and self-expression but it is also vulnerable to the apparent logic of intellectualisation and easily denigrated. In the same way the most callous acts of man can be justified by cold logic, as history has shown many times over.

Exercises in Reducing Intellectualisation

1 Try to observe yourself in this role. You will almost certainly not see yourself as being intellectual, but you may perhaps feel yourself as forceful or reasonable, over-bearing and controlling in certain 'justified' opinions towards others.

2 Try also to see when and why you become intellectual and with which people. There are almost certainly replica situations and patterns when you are controlling or imposing ideas to limit a situation and your own vulnerability. See if this happens in a situation where there is a particular threat or challenge, and if so what it is.

3 Clarify how you feel about people in general, how confident you really are and recall more secure situations, where you are less forceful, pressurising and rigid.

4 Try to go back to the origins of these attitudes and look for any clear cut reasons for intellectualising – perhaps where it 'paid-off' at one time.

5 Gently, with sensitivity, not logic or intellect, try to ease yourself into a more tolerant, less certain, less controlling frame of mind in a repetitive situation. Begin in the most obvious area and work towards the more difficult ones.

6 Refrain from being harsh, intellectual, or judgemental. Be tolerant and gentle with yourself, as you also begin to listen and be more tolerant with others.

7 Ask others to tell you how they see you, especially if you cannot yourself get any insightful glimpse into intellectualising behaviour.

8 Write your own personal, exercise here, making it as simple as possible.

Chapter two

The Importance of Psychology to Everyday Life

For all of us, without exception, it is the satisfaction, or positive expression of psychological needs, energies and drives which gives purposeful force and shape to life. They are the hidden dynamo-force behind every enthusiasm, interest and motivation as well as goals chosen and directions taken. Their fulfilment leads to satisfaction and a sense of achievement, more than an actual task or work completed. Suppression, denial, or deviation of psychological energy is responsible for lethargy, flatness, depression, and loss of satisfaction and energy, the common symptoms which together with tension and anxiety fill every doctor's surgery to overflowing.

The basic underlying psychological impulse is to give-out, fulfil, express, to create at every conceivable level of contact and relationship. There are other needs to take in, receive and to enfold. These psychologicals are inseparable from basic physical needs also, often the instinctual ones for food, warmth, sexuality, protection and survival.

There is no aspect of man or woman that does not contain the psychologicals in some form or other and give expression to them. Research using hypnosis, psychological case studies, psychodrama and psycho-analysis has clearly confirmed this and shown how we unconsciously develop psychological themes and concerns in many physical as well as psychological areas of our being.

This continuous satisfaction of psychological needs and instincts – directly through relationships and indirectly through symbols and art – is a basic part of man's expression and need. In spite of this, psychological awareness is still one of the most neglected areas of education and industry, with personal relationships rarely taken very seriously or given sufficient time and attention for their understanding and need. Dialogue, awareness and clarification are *basic* psychologicals, not extras, needed at times of stress, uncertainty or change to help resolve problem-areas of anxiety, fear or doubt which arise.

In health and times of happiness, man radiates an aura of ease and spontaneity. Reassuring non-verbal signals of trust and warmth are given out, that facilitate openness and acceptance, the development of secure, relaxed relationships. When free expression is blocked, from any cause – either recent or remote, the opposite occurs, with flatness, an absence of glow and clearly felt signals. Attitudes of mistrust, hostility and suspicion develop as fears and aggression block relaxation and limit contact, communication and openness.

Defining Health

Health is the ability to contain and cope with internal pressures, as well as external demands in a balanced way. It is doubtful if anyone is now totally free from stress-demands. They should not however be overwhelming or a major distraction from an overall position of balance and harmony. For some part of the day, most of us are under pressure in one form or other. It is important that such stress-demands are seen for what they are – an unfamiliar, unaccustomed situation and a challenge, and be dealt with realistically and quickly. They should not be seen, or allowed to become anything more. Certainly stress should not distort or become excessive, nor should it be totally suppressed. Stress currents when present and denied undermine health, relaxation and well-being. Because freedom from external stress is now largely theoretical, what matters is that they are dealt with as they arise and not given *undue* emphasis or depth. A modern definition of health must include being able to contain stress as a part of everyday life and work without it being a threat or an imposition. In this way confidence can be built up and a healthy balance transmitted to both the physical and emotional expressions.

Health is a free, flexible mind, not one which is rigid, dominated or preoccupied. No one should be a slave to a particular thought, problem, idea or difficulty.

In general, difficulties are a challenge and a signal for a change of outlook, perception and thinking, but not more than that. It is well-known that physical illness need not impair emotional balance and that optimism and humour are common in the face of the most daunting physical problems. A physical illness is often not felt as such a threat or demand, as an emotional issue, but much more as a problem that can be 'handed over' to the experts concerned without conflict or guilt. In addition, there is not the loss of esteem and self-worth, which can occur with a psychological problem.

True health implies a healthy body and mind. Physical disease, even physical treatment, can at times overwhelm the strongest, creating infantile, dependent and regressive patterns of behaviour. When this happens, there is usually a clear-cut psychological reason, often dating back to earlier experiences in infancy, rather than an actual physical reason for the vulnerability. Health implies freedom from dependency and addiction as well as from panic and fear. There is freedom from dis-ease, whatever the particular pressures and needs at the time, the ability to stay securely centred without a serious threat to identity. The hyphen in dis-ease implies an internal hyphen also, an inner split or division psychologically – and this needs to be healed in every case, to regain health and happiness.

Too much emphasis is often given to the physical with insufficient attention paid to deeper psychological needs, despite the general knowledge that the roots and foundations of vitality lie within both. An uneasy mind, full of conflicts, doubts and fears, can never be a relaxed one, really healthy, because at each turning of life's way, a new situation is inevitably changed into a crisis or a threat, instead of a challenge to inspiration, new learning and growth.

Emotions, Illness, and Modern Man

Emotions and feelings are present from infancy onwards as a natural reaction to life's daily vicissitudes, the physical as well as the psychological events. Emotional reactions occur at least from birth onwards and probably during pre-natal existence, expressing individual reactions to life's happenings, and interactions, according to mood, temperament, maturity and the level of demand and pressure. Emotion is essentially a heightened state of reaction in a particular area. It intrudes, seeks to impose and impress itself upon conscious happenings in a wide variety of ways as currents of strong feelings. They are stimulated by demand and encounter, enhanced by phantasy and past experience. At times they feel like an unwelcome guest, taking over, upsetting plans, draining energy, interfering to delay a commitment and decision-making. When this happens it is important to be able to separate the emotional facts of the matter from the realities, otherwise there is confusion and uncertainty which adds to any distress present.

Our pressurised society injects tension into every family as it is re-structured, and this can be a powerful negative stimulus to life and living because of the uncertainties, sense of vulnerability and fear. Where these are expressed as outbursts and violent protest, tension becomes worse because of fear of loss of control.

Because the social pressures are largely unexpected, new and radical they are unprepared for. Refusal, or the inability to make changes and adjustment leads to severe social and personal problems. New opportunities however potentially rewarding may be rejected in favour of futile attempts to retain old patterns and the familiar – because change is seen as a potential exposure to failure or loss.

Too often there is a tendency to stay in a 'dead end', known situation, rather than to make a shift and a psychological change which would allow an alternative new to be experienced. The risks are feared because of too little past experience or training in making changes.

Our educational system has in the past been far too traditional and closed, too fact and examination-orientated with few exceptions, offering little for a more flexible individual or creative approach to problem-solving. Insufficient time has been given to the possibility of learning and developing new alternative approaches and solutions so that coping with actual change or crisis is now totally new and unfamiliar. The development of such skills and confidence is nevertheless essential, to cope with and prepare for changes at every level so that new ideas and new thinking can emerge at a critical stage, rather than later in retrospect. Because of early specialization in schools and unimaginative routine attitudes, many are now highly vulnerable to the problems that change and modernisation bring. A crisis may occur because creative thinking and imaginative attitudes are not available at times of pressure and need. Panic and fear occur because of the psychological unreadiness, which paralyses thinking and inhibits a more flexible, imaginative approach to crisis and problem-solving.

The price paid for the lack of creative problem-solving is that tension and stress are increased by fear and inexperience, leading to wrong, rigid attitudes and attempts to impose old recipes to new problems.

Emotions are the outer waves of inner man, and stress is the prevailing wind – sometimes a gale which beats the waves into torment, creating 'highs and lows' of feeling. The very shores of equanimity can be threatened by such tides of emotion and natural safeguards of humour, imagination and experience swamped by overwhelming panic, despair, and fear. Stress-laden emotions are the product of external events, exaggerated and distorted by internal insecurity, leading to blockage and refusal to look at the realities. Lack of contact and perception because of the anxiety, overwhelms objective thinking. Too often, basic insecurity distorts a simple but unfamiliar situation into a critical one because there has been insufficient experience, confidence and resilience developed in the past to tolerate growth and change.

Women can be just as vulnerable as men in these areas especially when home, family and security are threatened. Less unrealistic than men in a crisis situation because of childbirth experience and their closeness to biological cycles, women can also distort reality under pressure and lose touch with their realities. In general it is the early infantile fears that race back to the surface at times of crisis, in order to dominate by the overwhelming force of the feelings and assumptions. They can threaten the whole fabric of stability and security for a time, especially where strength is more apparent than real. Breakdown or psychological collapse may occur if resilience is weak so that an unfamiliar situation becomes magnified into something impossible, with a creative, alternative solution seeming remote.

A secure background and a solid adult relationship give the best protection against such overwhelming stress currents. Where a problem has been denied or suppressed with a stubborn refusal to admit its existence, there is danger of sowing the seeds of a later psychological illness, especially depression, anxiety-tension and lack of confidence.

When emotional whirlpools become exaggerated and distorted by pressures, uncertainties and unknowns, they also feed earlier scars and conflicts, leading to increased neurotic phantasy. A psychological illness, like depression, tension, or phobia, is the crystallisation of such pressures, aggravated by ostrich attitudes of denial or fear and inflated by infantile magical assumption.

Illness is the outward expression of these inner processes, often present for years in a less acute, subdued form. Inner doubts frequently precede illness, long before distortions, blockage and paralysing problems occur. Panic or an obsessional illness is only the final act of self-limitation and denial after a long period of psychological preparation.

During the period of pre-crystallisation or pre-emergence of a physical illness, the individual has frequently been stiff and rigid in thinking, sometimes completely denying the existence of a hurt or problem. The combination of denial and suppression, living on the outside, rather than within, external stress and pressures, inadequate rest and a diet that is commercial rather than nutritional, drains physical and emotional reserves so that collapse or breakdown inevitably happens.

When psychological illness occurs, there has usually been insufficient time given for a significant personal contact in depth, with feelings and motivations. Relatives and friends usually know the reasons behind a breakdown or physical illness, the real areas of pain, sadness or loss. In some cases a family has colluded, to sweep the true causes under a psychological carpet of 'everything is alright, and nothing is wrong'.

For many, the emotions and feelings which make up the real self are devalued by matter of fact and superficial attitudes, into something for gossip or a chat. They become an external activity like taking a pill, rather than an occasion for calm thought, the admission of need and depth.

Alcohol is one of the commonest recipes to give a temporary respite from deeper problems. Others are gambling, cigarettes, irritability or violence. But whatever recipe is chosen, behind it, there is always denial, flight and suppression, with a preference for the outer, instant, rather than a change in depth. In most cases, the outcome is both temporary and ineffective. When the real areas of difficulty and feeling are admitted, the problem can be more easily resolved. Collusion between an individual and the family, usually means that neither faces up to the psychological realities of the situation – because they are uncomfortable. In the same way, the patient and his or her doctor may also collude, suppress or deny, so that a problem and the implications need not be diagnosed or looked at. In this way the internals grow to form blocks and more extensive problems, of a tangible physical nature because of obstruction to the changes required for a creative solution and psychological fulfilment.

Disease or Dis-ease?

More and more, people now realise that disease is not just something 'foreign' and external, that arrives one fine day and settles into the unsuspecting human host. It is now widely accepted that disease only occurs as the outcome of previous internal disharmony or disequilibrium, a process which prepares the soil for later invasion by physical agents of bacterial, viral, parasitic or other origin. Pain, weakness and degenerative changes are usually only later, secondary manifestations rather than primary causes of illness. Resistance and vitality are significantly reduced by imbalance within the psychological internals, long before any external manifestations appear. Before a definite physical disease occurs, there has often been malaise and discomfort, reflecting physiological disturbance and diminished function, as vitality is impaired. Once this takes place formerly symbiotic organisms in partnership, extend and proliferate, to take advantage of a weakened defensive energy flow, becoming secondary factors or invaders that further reduce and impair health.

The psychological internals are frequently suppressed feelings of an intense kind which both block and deny. Occasionally they breakthrough spontaneously and uncontrollably burst into external expressions as an outburst or flood of feelings. When this happens they are usually only allowed the briefest possible expression, and the break-through is quickly covered-up or forgotten and the psychological gains are minimal. There may also be some surfacing of feelings within a particular relationship, where irritability, intolerance, anger or fear are allowed out, as well as love and caring. There are often too few outlets for these disturbed feelings, because they are over-controlled and denied. Like the genii of the lamp, they are bottled-up, within a functioning physiological unit, and all the associated channels and organs then become vulnerable to its negative influence.

Atmospheric chemicals and wastes like lead, sulphuric acid, exhaust-fumes, vibration and noise all substantially diminish functioning and well-being by their direct toxic effect. With sensitive tissues, this sometimes leads to specific disease-patterns as in lead poisoning. Each is dangerous in its own way and more so, where the balancing psychological factors are under tension or stress.

Relationships and Modern Man

In order for the sensitive man or women to remain healthy, a consistent on-going personal relationship, with dialogue, sharing, contact and affection, is essential. Work and job satisfaction are important but they too need consistency, dialogue and response, to maintain them at a satisfying creative level. For this to occur, there has to be an open sharing of information, ideas, and feelings at personal levels. Discussion from planning stage onwards, with inter-consultation and sharing is fundamental, however simple or complicated the product or project in hand. This is an extension of personal caring and needs into the work area, the person feeling valued and appreciated as an individual, and not just 'a cog in a wheel', with no opportunity to give-out, suggest, discuss, disagree or respond.

Consideration, consultation and discussion are important and vital, both at home and in the work area. Both are necessary for personal satisfaction and also to evoke a creative response. Without dialogue and openness, little can develop or flourish, however inventive and motivated the individual. Trust, security and caring need to be fostered and fed by sensitive support, and a relationship that encourages expansion, the growth of new ideas, free expression, inspiration and creativity.

Self-expressions, Sharing and Talking

The significance of each meaningful contact relates to the degree of openness, sharing and recognition of the other. Opportunities for self-expression, the development of ideas, free association and a sharing of feelings are all basic to caring creative relationships, as well as to health and satisfaction. This gives an optimal backcloth for psychological expansion and physical development, so that interest and alertness can be kept maximal and a more individual expression and response made possible in every situation.

Without personal self-expression, there can be no real contact with others. Images of reality become distorted and twisted by a combination of assumption and phantasy into an unfriendly world of hostility and criticism. Although such assumptions may have a basis in reality, it is usually a phantasy-reality only. Nevertheless they impinge upon the whole organism, physically and emotionally draining health and confidence.

The intrusion of past pain and hurt into present day perception and understanding is always damaging. It can be clearly seen in a dog, abandoned and beaten as a puppy, who still chases every moving car or bicycle, because it is still under the influence of the earlier experience and damage. Fear of dentists in adults may also take origin in similar earlier traumas.

A woman of 40 had her face slapped as a child by an impatient dentist when she cried and complained of pain. Her adult dental fears clearly took her back to that time, with a combination of rage, hurt pride and anxiety which were at the origin of the adult fears. In some, such fears have been injected by others reflecting *their* problem, fears and attitudes but internalised at a time when vulnerability and suggestibility were maximal and not easy to expel later. This is common too in the fear of mice or small animals when the reactions of a parent are injected into the vulnerable mind of the developing child.

There is an unfortunate tendency to play and re-play old tapes from the past, in order to try to gain control over them and prevent their recurrence. But too often such psychological re-plays only serve to reinforce the past and its uncertainties, rather than overcoming them. The constant re-casting of yesterday's happenings in the present, does little to increase confidence, understanding or creative development. A repetitive preoccupation with old themes is rarely helpful, because it distorts and limits the present without significantly adding to growth, learning or reality experience.

It is essential to separate and distinguish a feared past experience, its memory and imagery, from assumptions about the present and interpretations of reality. Anything that helps lessen barriers and assumptions also frees associated emotional phantasies, In this way they can eventually blend and contribute positively into a more creative experience of the present, rather than negating it. Crying 'Wolf' before every situation and encounter is a recipe for frustration and failure in the present, and for fear and apprehension in the future.

Expanding Interests and an open Mind to Combat Neurosis

It is possible to define neurosis as the expression of a closed mind. All new experiences and expanding interests which stimulate broader attitudes are conducive to health. Interest in others supports this reality so that there are fewer assumptions, less phantasy-confusion of reality because there is less alienation. Contact with others is always a stimulus to new learning and each encounter has its message if listened to. Expanding interests means there is more to give out. As care and spontaneity develop, defensiveness and self-interest diminish. Contact is also essential for more open learning and growth, giving essential feed-back information and stimulation. All of this helps correct and balance the assumptions of a neurotic, closed inner world of primitive imagery and phantasy. When properly directed, meditation or prayer leads to greater contact with self and others provided that it is not seen as an end-result or an outlet for self-interest.

Exercises to Expand Interest and Awareness

1 Define your major areas of interest. See how these also may control you and to what extent. Clarify the degree to which you allow your interests to be flexible and varied. Change any aspects which are limiting to personal expansion and growth.

2 Look at other areas where you would like to be more involved, but which are not possible because of inconvenience, time, opportunity, availability etc. Start to make changes in spite of the difficulties listed and see them as a challenge to overcome. Begin to be more involved in those areas where you would like to be. Consider the barriers only as fences and hurdles of your own making, difficulties that you can alter and overcome.

3 Define any areas which you particularly dislike, things beneath you, too difficult or

impossible even to consider. Imagine and see yourself as participating in such areas. Feel their interest and enthusiasm. Experience their interest and understand why you resist them. Within the bounds of any physical limitations, participate more and in some way in these areas.

4 Try to see your own interest areas from a child's point of view. Enjoy them as if you were a child, with alertness, feeling and spontaneity. Next experience them as a teenager and the feelings associated with that time. Then as an adult, and note the difference. Try to see what feelings or spontaneity you have lost from the past and make contact with them again. Attempt to expand your own horizons, perceptions and enthusiasms in this way and learn something from every age.

5 Write your own exercise for expanding interests making it personal and specific.

Sensitivity awareness for Health

Awareness and sensitivity are the basic steps to knowledge and personal growth, stimulating psychological direction and motivation, lessening vulnerability. Meaningful contacts expand and develop. Superficial trivial ones lessen and limit. Awareness is sensitivity to each situation as it occurs and is fundamental to every healthy relationship. Awareness of personal strengths as well as weakness gives confidence, so that each situation can be responded to in a flexible way according to the needs and realities at the time.

Self-awareness is psychologically quite different from sensitivity-awareness, the individual less comfortable because of its self-orientated nature. Because it alienates from others, undermining depth and flexibility which are basic to every full personal contact, ease and relaxation are also considerably limited.

Sensitivity is staying in touch with the deeper psychological strands of every contact and involves self-knowledge, pain at times, awareness of feelings, motivations, directions and aims. It is inseparable from other-awareness and as feelings are much more accepted, there is heightened intuitive sensitivity. Such awareness maintains contact with conscious needs as well as the deeper feelings. Accepting needs as well as limitations and differences puts the individual in an optimum position to respond to each new and different contact with all their resources and a wide variety of different responses.

Exercises in Developing Sensitivity-awareness

1 Realise yourself as someone unique. Visualise the individual you are as successful, achieving the things you are aiming for. Note how imaginative you are in your general approach to a problem and how this could be varied Note any blocks, and that these reflect problems you yourself create, rather than any intrinsic to the situation. See how your attitudes, assumptions and expectations relate to reality and help find solutions. Note how the *successful* you approaches a problem and how differently it can be understood and worked at. Aim now to clear any impasses, non-sequiturs and blind alleyways that you are creating. Identify and act much more as the achieving, successful and visualising you in every approach to problems. Stop re-enacting and repeating the old failure-pattern of the past.

2 See how well-trodden paths of attitude and viewpoint make for difficulties. Now start to use them more positively, to widen and open-up perception areas which you have not been admitting.

3 Use the 'brainstorming' principle of approaching a problem or difficulty by a spontaneous flow of ideas as they occur – realistic or otherwise. Write them all down without assessing or judging them as to their relevance, value or reality. Just let the ideas and associations flow out of you without analytic or judgemental comment on what you have produced. This may be done with another person if you prefer, both recording the totality of ideas that emerge. Use specific new ideas to improve blind spots and no-go areas. Retain others of interest and stimulus although they seem to have no immediate value in the present, as pointers to future direction and growth.

4 See how many of your attitudes and ideas originate from within yourself, or are artificially induced by your social group, family, upbringing and education. Look back at earlier aims and ideals too – as you were then, and how much you may have come to resemble the pack. It may help to think back to when you first started school, university, or a first job. See how much of yourself you have allowed to become programmed and motivated by others – their wishes, their expectations and their

motivations. Clarify how far you have deviated, rather than grown from your original, more authentic self, ideals, and beliefs. See yourself, as you would like to be now. Note how much or how little of the earlier lost ideals you would retain. Work out a method and a schedule to recapture and to re-unite with lost ideals, aims and values which you still see as important and relevant.

5 Create a new exercise for yourself in sensitivity-awareness. Write it down after these comments. It must be a practical one that you can develop and use.

Caring for Others to Combat Narcissism and Self-interest

The experience of giving-out is as important as receiving and feed-back. Listening to others is vital for positive psychological health and its development. Negative feelings – of anger, resentment, withdrawal, exasperation or exhaustion are to some extent an inseparable part of your psychological totality. They should not however be predominant unless there is a clear reason for it. Ambivalence of feeling, doubt and trust are also unavoidable and a normal part of life's duality, the essential shadow-image of the positive and inseparable from it. Self-love is positive, provided that it is not entirely and primarily narcissistic and leads to greater caring and appreciative consideration for others.

Caring for others is an expression of loving and leads to greater closeness, belonging, fulfillment and happiness. In this way the higher sides of man develop and strengthen, with greater sensitivity to needs and feelings, lessening self-interest and self-indulgence. All of this contributes to better health, maturity and more creative satisfaction. Caring for others is also caring for the self because every experience of loving enriches.

Exercises in Caring

1 Think of the needs of someone close, imagine yourself as them, how they feel, as they see you. Sense their needs. Do this first for a person you like and feel close to. Then the same exercise for someone you like less or are less safe with. On each occasion try to see and feel how the other sees you and why. Try to acknowledge the positive aspects of a person you dislike as also the faults and weaknesses of someone you like. In either case, see the needs of the other, and how you can meet these in a more positive way.

2 Next visualise yourself, interacting with both sets of people, and see yourself from an outsider's viewpoint – how you are in action with their different personalities. See yourself in disagreement with a person you like and in harmony with someone you dislike. Try to understand why and how you have grouped them differently and why you place them at opposite poles. Does this relate to ways you categorise people in general? Clarify the steps which you can take to develop these relationships and then repair them after a dispute. See caring clearly developing after a negative situation as well as within a positive one.

3   Start to give out more in reality situations, to those you like and dislike. Give in terms of time, listening, interest, compassion and understanding, not concretely or materially. Give to those you feel negative towards, as well as to those who matter. Try to control and limit judgemental, condemning, moralising attitudes at the same time. Strong likes may deny ambivalent non-giving just as a strong negative reactions frequently cover positive feelings. Start now, in reality to identify with and understand the needs of others. As you give out to them, sense yourself interacting, but don't be an onlooker within a relationship of caring. Don't be afraid of appearing negative, to disagree or be different, as long as you are being you – as you feel and experience, at the time.

4   See how you yourself are limiting giving and caring and what aspects of yourself, you withold. At the same time understand how this limits you. Clarify any assumptions and prejudices about others which you use to justify the witholding.

5   Look at the areas where you are able to give out more. See yourself giving to those close to you. Do it also in reality. See how others care for you. Feel their caring and why it is important.Understand just what it means and why it matters. See their needs too, at the same time as your own.

6 Create an exercise for greater giving and caring which relates to you at present. Write it down and put it into action now.

Sharing and Trust for Greater Understanding of Others

Every shared experience, even that of pain, ultimately strengthens. It gives strength because giving to another is the most powerful positive experience possible, and sharing is giving. The building-up of closeness leads to greater confidence and experiences, which increase self-knowledge. Sharing inevitably extends trust, the processes of identification and internalisation which build-up a confident internal reality that can give out to others. Discernment, judgement and discrimination are important aspects of sensitivity-awareness and growth. As phantasy-fear currents are diminished by reality contacts, trust and sharing, healthy meaningful relationships are also increased by it. These contacts are essential for creative expression, and to give a secure base for feed-back and the inter-play of ideas and associations. Sharing implies understanding and a viewpoint that accepts the other as a changing different human being, with the right to have a different point of view. Change is basic for life and growth rather than a barrier to it. Sharing helps to see that problems are often common difficulties which are not so isolated or unique as is often feared. A difficulty can be a key or stimulus to resolving other problems and in this way a positive stimulus to insight, growth and change.

Sharing should not be seen as the passive unloading of problems into an accepting other. It involves a much more active process, of staying in touch with needs, priorities and feelings. Listening, a positive attempt to gain perspective, and a spontaneous response gives confidence, and with it a lessening of anxiety.

Exercises in Sharing and Trust

1 Visualise clearly the people you share with at present. Sharing means of your real self, – aims, thoughts and feelings. Clarify also those you are deliberately not sharing with.

2 Try to see your reasons for giving to some and not to others. See where and how you limit, and your divisions of sharing and giving.

3 Understand more clearly the 'easy' relationships where you give out more of yourself. Now see where you give less in a more limited, defensive way.

4 Visualise yourself as giving out spontaneously to both groups. First, giving out thoughts and ideas, then feelings, love and caring. See where you limit and when, and how you cut off. Clarify those moments

clearly and any precise areas where you limit and hold back. Understand why you do this.

5 Start to give out more to those you are already close to. These may include friends, family, or work colleagues. Be more attentive, patient, caring, and more careful. Be more of a listener as well as a giver to the real needs. See yourself extending this into other contacts you meet, not just the close ones.

6 See which people you trust and feel able to give, relate to, and care about. Clarify what it is you like and trust about them. With others whom you dislike or hold back from, see where and how you can move more towards them, understanding their needs as people. Don't wait for them to make the first move. See those you dislike as vulnerable, individuals with feelings and needs just like your own.

7 See yourself expanding in the areas where you withhold and allow this to happen in reality as you slowly feel and visualise the changes.

8 Create your own individual exercise next for this area. Write it down, then act on it.

Listening to Combat Avoidance Talking

Talking to avoid or to erect barriers is common, especially where there is the fear of not coping well, with a sudden or unexpected situation. It is often a reflection of not wanting to know or to be involved in the feelings and needs of others – from either fear or indifference. The drive to shut-out, alienate, not to feel, experience, or know in cases of need is a very common one.

Listening to others, like any form of true closeness means feeling, identifying and experiencing both the self as well as the other. The re-experiencing of strong feelings may be unwelcome and a source of anxiety. Nervous talking which is largely superficial, can often be based on ambivalence or avoidance, in case there is an awareness of need or a demand for change. Such talking gives no space or pause for real issues to emerge. The basic motivation is to stay on the outside, on the surface, rather than sensitive and listening in depth. Words can be a barrier as much as a communication to any relationship. Listening with an open mind leads to more understanding, less contracted rigid viewpoints, more open attitudes and spontaneous giving. Quick talk and fast chatter, without direction or meaning, lacks depth and motivation, other than avoidance and staying superficial. Listening can overcome the barriers that words, reason and emotion erect defensively. Quiet, dynamic listening means awareness of need and depth, staying alert to others without judgement or loss of identity.

Exercises in Listening and Experiencing Others

1 Listen more to yourself – when you are quiet and at peace but also when you are animated and active. Daily, give yourself a 15-minute quiet period to practise your own internal listening. Don't judge or comment on any thoughts or feelings, just listen. Don't be overwhelmed, and listen in stillness.

2 Listen also to others close and near to you. Try to see at what point you get tired and irritable, or become over-talkative and block them. See when and how you shut others off. Also why you do this, and consider asking others how they experience and feel about it at the time.

3 Start to listen more to others less close to you. This may be easy and obvious, but not less important. As you listen, identify with them, their needs, underlying communications, the essential of each person and

their basic feelings. This does not mean becoming them or being taken over. You are aiming at greater depths of understanding to becoming more flexible, less assumption-dominated and blocking. See where you can give-out more at a deeper, rather than surface level. See the true needs and real levels of each communication. Try not to be deflected from them and respond at that level whenever possible.

4 See any areas you are blocking and avoiding. Clarify how these may block-off others who you need and also who need a greater closeness with you.

5 Look at the areas where you are most enthusiastic, interested and attentive. See if these are at all a defence or absorbing alter-native to more challenging new involve-ments which you avoid from fear, or resistance to change.

6 Write down your own exercise next. It should always be individual, relating to your attitudes and needs in the particular area.

Chapter three

Security

Security is the underlying strength of personality that gives the outward confidence to express, relate and explore. In each and every individual without exception, security is the key factor to personality development and a major one in attaining mature adulthood. Excessive psychological pressure, physical damage or trauma can seriously displace security, provoking neurotic reactions, so that its direct expression is lost or unavailable. In this way much of the joy of life is lost or at half-measure. Neurosis and insecurity are the end-result of such withdrawal and phantasy rather than a creative expression of existence and being.

Security gives a sense of wholeness that comes from an integration of drives, personality and basic needs. Reassurance however, never gives true security and at best is a temporary boost to confidence rather than a source of inner strength. Inner security creates the right psychological conditions for outer security, for growth, sensitivity and receptivity to others.

Security gives a sense of personal presence and recognizable identity, so that contacts and relationships occur in a climate of trust. It facilitates personal growth allowing a greater experience of the self with others and more original reactions to life's changing scenes and challenges.

When there has been no undue early damage or trauma, security is present from birth and clearly seen in the youngest child at the bottle or breast. It is expressed as confident drives and the earliest expressions of need, demand and assertion. The secure baby complains, rages and cries as well as gurgles, smiles and sleeps. The insecure infant is much more limited in personal expressions and is already more stereotyped in its cry, movements, and explorations. Self-awareness exists from the earliest weeks onwards, at the same time as awareness of others. As security builds up, together with confidence, there is greater spontaneity of expression in a variety of physical as well as psychological ways.

Security gives the background, and confidence for spontaneity of action, decisiveness, and exploration within the spectrum of everyday happenings, so that a varied expression and response can occur. These also lead to change and growth in more adventurous creative ways at every age, and being more active and outward. Much of this is taken for granted, yet security is undoubtedly one of man's most precious as well as abused gifts.

From birth onwards, security is necessary for healthy growth and is the basis for stimulating a vitality which gives the overall shape and resilience to every experience and self-expression. Whenever hurts and frustrations occur, they can be made more tolerable and acceptable when seen in a more real perspective.

Security allows self-confidence to develop, expanding curiosity and knowledge with enjoyment and pleasure. Especially it supports the growth of an overall sense of cohesiveness and togetherness which prevents the development of personality disorganisation which may lead to schizoid or hysterical problems. Security helps combat the tendency to deny reality challenges and difficulties by splitting, fragmenting or projecting them away from awareness, so that eventually an unreal phantasy-imaginative world dominates reality. Security is a basic factor in the development and maintainence of health at every age, level of maturity, or prevailing stress at the time.

The unconscious-equivalent of a safety-valve, it helps to contain and tolerate anger and pressure-situations without reactions of short-fuse rage and loss of control, because the pressures and unknowns can be more easily accepted. Lack of security leads to anxiety, excessive reactions of overwhelming emotional response, as the demands and realities of everyday situations are turned into threats and pressures.

Security is the most important psychological principle behind every authentic self-expression, giving the freedom to assert, act and to be spontaneous. When confident and secure, the individual is able to express and apologise, but it may be impossible to be spontaneous later, when the occasion has passed. Security and confidence are needed to be able to make mistakes, to be wrong, and to admit it. Only by tolerating mistakes can new learning occur. Insistence on being right, correct and perfect all the time is unhealthy and unreal, serving only to hide weakness or lack of confidence and it is ultimately a blockage to growth.

A contemporary song says − 'the nearest thing to heaven is a child'. This may be true for the psychologically healthy child, but for the damaged infant, being a toddler can also be the nearest thing to hell, especially when security is weak or absent.

Security supports the ability to give, to act spontaneously and to respond to each different situation that occurs, however varied, without reducing it to narrow rigid perception or pattern. It supports coping with criticism and challenges as they occur. A tense, held-in attitude, gives little strength or self-reliance because tension increases withdrawal, suppression, alienation and fear.

A father's recent comment on his bright four-year old was – "She's full of life, vigour and cheek". Certainly vigour, spontaneity and audacity are hallmarks of security with a willingness and a pleasure to face challenge and change. Each new situation, from starting school, to a first visit to the doctor or dentist should be of interest and part of life's expanding experiences. It should not be a threat or occasion for overwhelming emotion – unless it is the product of an earlier trauma or mismanagement. Security is ultimately freedom of self-expression – because it supports physical and psychological momentum, the ability to change, adapt and give out whatever the pressures and realities of the situation.

Dependence, even inter-dependence on others, and awareness of need make for vulnerability, in some degree. Strength and security lie in being able to accept dependency need as well as vulnerability. As security grows so too does human frailty and vulnerability and these needs must be acknowledged.

As one patient put it recently,"Insecurity feels like driving on a motorway with no hard shoulder". Loss of security gives rise to the fear of having no escape routes, a sense of a paralysing imminent collapse. Acute loss of security leads to acute anxiety and acute fears. Only when these have been eradicated, put into balance, can security be re-established. But whatever the fears or pressures, security is never totally destroyed, although at times it seems lost to awareness, availability and knowledge. When this happens, security is hidden and unconscious, until less threatening times appear, or a positive psychological change has occurred which allows it to re-surface.

Security takes origin in genetic as well as in environmental factors. In a single-parent family, grandparents and other adult contacts are important alternative figures to identify with during childhood and adolescence. These play a role in personality development, forming its roots and layers, building flexibility and re-silience into sensitivity and feeling as long as the experiences have been positive, consistent and reliable. Fear, doubt, loss or rejection, can turn the experiences into an opposite negative one. In this way, layers of variable strength and weakness are formed from the early ex-ploratory contacts. Security grows at the same time as the taking-in of closeness, self-expression and contact. Such human basics give the foundation for all future balance, later explorative drives, more open creative thinking and adult maturity. Security is fed by feelings of being valued, appreciated and needed, but most of all it is nurtured by needing and caring. The experience of being loved gives comfort and reassurance, but only loving gives a depth to security.

The giving-out and sharing of a vulnerable self, creates confidence, growth and strength. Receiving even of love and caring, is at best a 'holding' measure, a temporary source of reassurance, leading to some weakness because of the dependency engendered. Giving to others does not create such problems, nor does it weaken and undermine ego (self) strength.

The regular elimination of negative, failure-ideas and feelings is as important psychologically as it is physically. We need psychological 'bran' – confidence, trust, sharing and security as much as vegetable fibre to prevent the retention of blocking emotions – especially fear and resentment which put security at risk. Where there has been a recent trauma or pressure, perhaps problems of tension and insomnia, then healthy elimination is even more important. In the child such elimination occurs quite naturally through play, chatter, phantasy and dreaming. But if emotional elimination is blocked, the stage is set for loss of spontaneity, stagnation of confidence and the retention of anxiety.

The insecure person can also show the most amazing strength and determination, once he knows the setting, environment and permitted boundaries. Security is the ultimate key to each psychological situation and challenge. Although security cannot be obliterated by pressures or fears, it can be withdrawn from availability – and this is when problems occur or panic may set in.

Examples of Security in Various Age-Groups

1 A few weeks ago I watched a child of eighteen months. He was confidently walking, able to move with tottering enjoyment, sure of himself as he climbed in and out of his pushchair. At one point he walked up to another tiny tot, pushed his face close to her's and stared. Equally cool and secure she watched and stood her ground. Then just as suddenly, he ran back to his mother, clambered into his chariot and calmly waited for her to complete the shopping chores.

A baby of six months was brought to the clinic with teething problems. Both parents were highly verbal communicating people and the child had already benefited from this. He was advanced for his age, stood well, listened and looked, wanting to walk, talk and to learn. He crawled vigorously trying to touch or mouth as he explored. Appetite and energy were enormous. His mother complained that he would not sleep and was demanding, making talking noises most of the night which exhausted them both. She wanted help with his sleeping, to see if there was any way he could be encouraged to settle more easily at night. There were however no problems with confidence and security – these were already well established.

Enraged by his painful gums, the child loudly and obviously complained whenever he was put down, as he was equally exasperated by anything which hampered his movements. Determined to reach any attractive object, he was a mixture of drive and frustration, hungering for food, as well as for objects – demanding to know, feel, touch, taste, experience. Protests were a loud mixture of anger, pride and indignation. Although only just upright, he clearly stated 'I want, I am' as he balanced precariously with both feet and one hand. Psychological security and curiosity were well in advance of physical co-ordination and because this lagged behind, became a cause of continual frustration.

2 Security can also be seen in healthy older children of eight or nine. Full of endless play and energy, they only cease their confidences, questions, tears and laughter for a quick snack, playing and moving in a ceaseless demand for feed-back, attention and new experiences. They confidently compete for adult attention as well as their peers. At other times they may be quietly absorbed in a book, puzzle or television, then suddenly spring into lively activity or collapse from fatigue. School, friends, interests, hobbies all reflect the effervescent emergence of energy, drive and confidence.

3 In the balanced teenager, the expression of security continues as confident activity and trendy intense involvements. There is no stopping of back-chat, knowing, opinions and

plans as a major expression of high energy and excitement. An expanding identity finds expression, style and outlet in a wide variety of interest. Group activities are the rule, with a healthy opposition to conventional ideas, patterns and adult priorities which they often quite correctly perceive as uncreative. Intense love and hate are other parts of the platform which security explores at this stage. The brash, sometimes provocative insensitive attitudes can also be as uniform and standard as the adult imagery which they seek to overturn, as they slowly raise themselves into adulthood, with a more balanced overall perspective and mature identity.

4 Security in the adult accepts the need for adjustment, responsibility and change without undue protest or denial. Challenge, stress, and pressures are seen in less dramatic terms, more as alternatives for discussion and action, however inconvenient or unwelcome, rather than reasons for disaster, breakdown, flight or illness.

Examples of Insecurity in Different Age Groups

1 Where security is absent at an early age, there is quite a different picture from the secure infant. The damaged child may be found

alone, rocking, remote and distant in a vain rhythmic attempt to find calm and peace. At other times head-banging occurs in a meaningless repetitive way, against the side of the cot or bed in search of a crumb of familiarity and comfort. The world seems an unfamiliar, unfriendly place, with adults who either abandon, or inflict pain and frustration. The over-whelming priority is to keep experiencing and re-experiencing the weakened self-identity structure over and over again, by repetitive physical actions, to gain some reassurance of existence and being.

2 The insecure child is shy and clinging, either less openly demanding, or seeking attention by excessive demands. Usually fearful, they lack the confident provocation and flamboyant seductiveness of the secure child. Physical drive and energy spurts may be absent, or too controlled, and checked by neatness, order and perfection. When the obsessional tendencies are strong, the patterns and rituals may be repeated endlessly.

3 The insecure teenager is often a loner who fails to rebel or to be openly provocative in any direction. He may also be a fringe member of a violent, anti-social group. Generally a conformer within a particular group, in some ways he or she seems old before their time. Sulky and unhappy, the insecurity causes frequent complaints and they are less likely to laugh or effervesce with enthusiasm and drive. There are usually too few real friends, too many

uncertainties, so that joy and fun are kept at a whining, complaints level, which is not seen so much in the secure teenager. Especially lacking, are the sudden rewarding exposures of humour and fun, and their absence is a major cause of sadness, anxiety or moodiness.

4 The insecure adult complainingly clings to the same job, the same relationships, the same marriage or lack of it – for reasons of routine and safety rather than from a caring commitment and involvement. Under the surface are powerful ambivalent negatives, but rarely expressed directly. These may emerge as repetitive, physical problems of a grumbling, incurable nature – chronic pains, indigestion, exhaustion or constipation. There may be more obvious psychological phobic problems, involving travelling, eating out in public, or going out, so that they prefer to stay protected and safe rather than in contact and aware of others. Insecurity always limits in some way, and at the same time, underlying negative attitudes towards others, who are seen as a threat, constantly create difficulties, and feelings of alienation. They are not usually happy in their job, life-style or with friends, because they cannot give-out enough to feel fulfilled – and what is given is often negative, complaining, or repetitive.

How to Combat Loss of Security

Make a start by being more honest with yourself. Go back to basic feelings, your *real* self, away from the usual patterns and attitudes which distort or limit you. By going back to basics, in this way, you may begin to see the start of the pathway which led you into patterns of withholding and blockage. See clearly how you initially lost security, and any related 'events' or traumas. Date these as far as possible.

Try going back, seeing yourself as you were – before security was lost. Get back into a more original position again, to healthier psychological foundations. Both self-negation and feelings of self-denial are anti-growth blocks to change and maturation. Controlling violence and keeping greed more in check is positive and supports change. Fixation on and preoccupation with the past can never lead to significant change because its aim is to prevent and control alternatives rather than to experience, react and respond in the present. However hurt you have been, you will always find the need to make some alterations in yourself although this may seem difficult at the time. You may not have changed enough from the time of an earlier hurt or loss, which still keeps you psychologically inert. Remember that events cannot paralyse, only their associated fears and feelings. Start by endeavouring to live more in the moment, in the present, being yourself as you are now, not according to past assumptions and imagery. Eradicate fears of the present which are based on assumption and phantasies of the past. Give-out and share much more of yourself, especially more of your spontaneity, caring, and interest.

Guidelines to Increasing Security

1   The best initial attitude is to accept that in spite of past hurts, you have survived, albeit scarred. But inside you are still yourself, however unexpressed, weak, muddled, frightened and resentful. You are still you, although hurt and damaged on the surface. Inevitably there is a scar, which you must carry with you, but your aim should be to rebuild in the now, and not to relive an ungrateful past in the present. See more – what and how you are now in the present, rather that how you might have been if the past had been different.

2   Living, expanding and expressing here and now, is the key to happiness, health, security and creative living, Accept both

love and hate, as inevitable, but above all live and be in the now.

Where trauma and damage are not in the past, but happening now, in the present, then you must distance yourself as soon as possible, so that physical and psychological oppression is minimal. You will need to change or improve the present environment in order to minimise damage and to create a more tolerable situation. This is essential, so that basic security can bud and grow again. Distancing may seem difficult or impossible, but often it is a change of attitude that is needed, more than a change of situation. Distance yourself from existing unbearable pressures to survive, grow and to live. There will always be some pressures, some stress. However bad and painful the past, at least a key remnant of you has survived, and this can later be developed into fuller expression, in a healthier environment. How do I know about this fragment? How can I be sure? Work with emotional illness clearly shows this healthy, residual fragment. Even in the most disturbed psychotic problems, there is a nucleus of health which remains, and can at times relate healthily, even understand and grow, given the right treatment and psychological environment.

3 To have lost security, you were probably hurt, bruised or damaged at a vulnerable time. You may have been held back or

deprived, but not destroyed as a person. Your scars are those of life's battle. Damaged perhaps and hurt, nevertheless you have survived and grown physically and psychologically since then. With less pressures, you may now be able to move on and out. Use the book to develop the insight to make a move towards a deeper understanding of self, others, and reality.

4 Scars give a depth, and a breadth of experience. They should not be resented. You probably would not wish to repeat the experiences, could have done without them, and probably feel that they were needless and a testimony of bad experience only. But begin to think more positively and see the past not only as negative. Look also for the positive spin-offs, however small. You would of course, have preferred no scars at all, but this is a *phantasy* for everyone. There is no growing-up without scars, however idealised the past, idyllic the surrounding. Some hurt is inseparable from maturity and gives a learning and a lesson which should not only be seen as negative and bitter. What matters now, is not past pain, but who you are now. It is your attitude to the present that matters most. Accept that you cannot put the clock back. Some people have a mission in life – to make others conform, to control and impose negatives upon them. Learn to sense and avoid such negatives as much as possible, to prevent them provoking imbalance and distress in the future.

5   Learn to develop less of a sensitive, soft centre, and more of a firm one in the coming months. In general avoid and distance yourself from anyone who is clearly out of tune with your personal aims and ideals, or who tries to tell you *who* to be, however close or family they are. Others may be trying to feel better at your expense, by getting you down. Prevent this happening also. Forget the past, even if you cannot understand or forgive it. Make time to make changes. Maturity only comes with time, determination, and the confidence to let go of a painful past. It may not be easy, but it is essential.

6   Begin by letting go of any strong intense feelings of resentment because these are the most undermining blocks to psychological growth. Lack of forgiveness and ingratitude are psychological inhibitors to growth, which foster hardness, sometimes rigid patterns which impede development.

7   Learn to live now and move ahead of the past into the present with definite plans for enjoyment, action and appreciation. Start to be again, even if for the first time in your life. But start now, not tomorrow. The ultimate solution to insecurity is giving, being and acting in the now.

Further Guidelines for Reducing Insecurity

1   Understand the roots and causes, with as much clarity and as little emotion as possible. Typical examples are an over-protected early life, an oppressive education, physical disability, or any acute loss or grief experience in the early vulnerable years. It is often associated with parental insecurity. Other common causes are separation at a vulnerable time, or loss of self-esteem and self-value following a psychological rejection. The other common psychological reasons are trauma of any kind, sexual interference, assault or aggression. Society itself may impose guilt and fear as with shame about sexuality or masturbation, usually associated with a repressed, rigid upbringing. Sudden illness, hospitalisation, a period of isolation without warning or explanation, can also lead to loss of security. All or any of these experiences may bring about insecurity by the absence of feeling valued or cared about.

2   **Negative Certainty**

This is important because it can perpetuate insecurity as well as other negative patterns over a lifetime. It usually presents itself as a sense of overwhelming certainty and conviction of failure, and being unloved, or that some disaster or negative is imminent. Such feelings lessen with healthy contacts and moves that expand or give-out a more spontaneous self expression.

3 Negative-specific Thoughts

These are extensions of negative certainty and need to be clearly understood in order to resolve insecurity problems. A theme or idea is repeated throughout the day or night, sometimes quite consciously and when combined with negative certainty creates the ideal conditions for the retention and repetition of a specific weakness problem. Once recognized and understood, they can be gradually lessened but much of the time they are an unconscious habit, dominating even sleep and dreams. Your own individual thought-negatives may contain some of the following examples, but whatever you find, record them at once for clarification of how you are reinforcing negatives and repetitive patterns.

Common examples are:– I cannot; I am deficient in some ways; I am less than others; I am not attractive; I am a failure; I have not achieved; I cannot succeed; I am unhappy; I am weak; I am ugly; I shall never; I could never; I shall never be able to. He or she is better, brighter, younger, wiser, healthier, etc, etc, etc – than I.

Essential Exercises for the Development of Greater Security

A major aspect of insecurity is the conviction that there is no cure or resolution for it. There may be a cure for others – you admit, but certainly not for you and that is why you cannot change. This certainty of being incurable is a specific negative thought in itself, which makes the beginning or starting of any change or endeavour pointless, defeating it before change gets a chance. Look for similar negatives in yourself from the onset. Hear them, but don't let them dominate you in any way as you work through the book and the exercises and as you begin to change.

1 Begin by clarifying your major positive areas, those where you are most secure. Build out from these. Start with people and situations where you are most comfortable and confident – perhaps at work, with friends or within your own family and home. Map out clearly all the positive, strongest aspects of yourself which you can think of. Positive areas exist in everyone, however unexpressed and insecurity is always a variable, fluctuating state. No one is insecure in every area all the time, and the most insecure individual has some areas of strength and confidence. You need to see

these clearly, to acknowledge and expand them, forming a platform and starting point for growth.

2   Having clearly defined the positive areas, now do the same for your weakest most vulnerable ones. Write down any fear or insecure areas, of limited self-expression or phobic inhibition. Especially note any additional pressures which may expand negatives, like crowds, having to wait, menstruation, climate, time of day etc. Try to understand why these factors add to anxiety.

3   Next look for areas of overlap, where you can build and extend the positive confident you into vulnerable limited areas. If you look carefully, you will find where you are both secure at times as well as totally lacking in confidence at others. These overlap areas are significant, and need to be understood. Start by slowly expanding and expressing yourself more in the overlap situations. You should find several areas of relative ease as well as uncertainty. Begin on a 'good', more relaxed day, rather than a 'bad', tense one. Try to extend and express yourself with more spontaneity, being more yourself. Be more you, but don't try however to be anyone else – to be you is enough. Aim to be less defended and less safe, above all say what you think, feel and mean.

On a 'bad' off day make no attempts initially at innovation or change. Just observe yourself quietly and learn from how you behave with others. If there are only 'off' days and no 'good' days – then this is clearly a pattern of defence against change. Look again to find times when you are less pressurised, able to make a start at more open self-expression, having first paved the way as above. As you improve, begin to make slight alterations and corrections in the insecure you. Eventually, work in different areas for short periods every day, whatever the feelings. Initially keep yourself to areas of overlap, until you build up confidence and then expand outwards from there.

4 Try to clarify any associated phantasies which inhibit you – your psychological running-commentary on life, to see how and to what extent it affects your approach to others, the sort of image, communication and non-verbal signals you give out. These are often anticipatory, programmed, phantasies, but with no relationship to reality. Record the phantasies and clarify their relevance and function trying to see why they are still on the psychological payroll.

Be scrupulously honest and open in your thinking about each area to avoid the threats – both emotional and infantile, behind each paralysing self-comment. Try to see for how long they have been present, and how they first became part of your everyday contact and expression, taking over life and spontaneity. See how this commentary has reinforced negative (doubting) certainties. In general their function is to limit and paralyse, rather than to support change and growth, by provoking uncertainty and fear.

5 Avoid over-concentration on the symbolic, apparent 'meaning' of such negatives. This may lead you into too much intellectual considerations and away from their essential *raison d'etre*. Ask trusted friends how they see and experience you, as long as they do not simply reassure and placate you. Use their imagery of you as a part of the overall picture, if you can use it positively. Be discriminating as you work out a new picture of relationships and how you limit, control or distort. Note the areas where you are confused, frightened or uncertain and see how you are creating them, by not allowing the light of reality to clarify confusion and to give you feed-back. Try to sense each outer reality occurrence as objectively as possible, without prejudging it or yourself. Negative certainty combined with negative thought imagery can create a perceptual system of apparent conviction, validity and 'truth' which is so paralysing and devastating that you cease functioning altogether.

6 Talk to others, without imposing or being boring, about insecurity and how they resolve it. Don't present it as an insolvable problem. Keeping it secret preserves much

of its apparent power and strength because it feeds on phantasy, alienation and fear. Overcome any feelings that it is not something to be shared or talked about. Insecurity is not something to be ashamed about. Everyone shares and knows it to some degree, and it is essential that such 'closed' psychological areas be made 'open' and available, more matter-of-fact, and more ordinary.

It is important too that you more fully experience others, aware of their inner doubt areas which they experience and have resolved. Being more open as well as available you will find support and understanding by giving to and sharing with others. No one is alone and unique in their problem. Fears reflect the human dilemma, they are not something to feel guilt, or ashamed about.

7   Create your own positive specifics, writing them down as counter-suggestions to the negative ones which feed and increase negative certainty. Use these daily for as long as the negatives are present – controlling and undermining you. Once the negatives have ceased or are quieter, repeat them only from time to time when needed. Be prepared to change a positive specific as you develop or whenever a new specific negative conviction attempts to limit you in any way.

Examples of Positive Specifics

Positive certainties are a specific affirmation to counteract negative certainty patterns. For example, if a specific negative certainty thought insists – 'I am no good'. 'I am unattractive', start the opposite affirmation, 'I am attractive'. Affirm the opposite strongly, specifically and often. Be quite specific and accurate and make a detailed note of any negative certainties so that you can oppose, check and correct them. Don't enter into intellectual argument as to whether or not your positive affirmation is true, this is not relevant to its function. You must believe it, but you are not using it for reassurance. Always use a personal specific-positive, otherwise you will be working on reassurance alone which is different, and of less value and relevance than your own specific.

8   Write down your own exercise for security building here. It should be different from any of the above and specifically related to your own needs, aims and individuality.

Chapter four

Fears and Modern Man

Fear is never the 'norm' for anyone. But where there is intolerable pressure, danger or threat, then fear naturally develops as a very positive 'alarm' function, mobilising adrenalin and the liver's glycogen energy reserves for fight or flight when needed. There is a surge of circulatory flow, to cope with an anticipated or actual emergency, with increased muscular and cardiac output. In most situations however, rather than being an instinct in the service of preservation and safety, fear is largely a negative pattern or habit which limits growth. It is predominantly a defence against change, closeness and contact with others because of the threat of being overwhelmed by a new or unfamiliar situation.

Neurotic fear is the product of tension within an unstable environmental or social situation. Often there is intimidation and more or less subtle pressures to change, to be different or to be someone or something else in order to be acceptable and loved. From earliest childhood, we are taught to conform to media, educational, family and cultural models, in order to be loved, successful and modern. If we don't conform to these patterns, we may be made psychologically redundant, economically too, especially when the demands are stringent and unbending.

For many it is the intimate pressures and models, those of the parents and family rather than the social ones which cause most tension. There is a great deal of pressure to conform to standardised ideals and images creating tension and fear. These suggestions or models, of how we should be, dress and play, impose false identities, as well as anxiety when they are not adhered to.

Neurotic fear is the outcome of overwhelming psychological attitudes of threat, loss or failure, precipitating primitive and rigid magical imagery into present day reality, although its roots lie in the past. In this way each contact, communication or meeting becomes distorted, a trigger to the re-emergence of a frightening past rather than a stepping stone into a stimulating present and a confident future.

The Causes of Neurotic Fear

External Factors

Any severe environmental pressure can deplete vitality and resistance. Typical examples are excesses of heat, cold, noise, vibration, over-crowding or exhausting travel. Working in any environment with high levels of atmospheric pollution, especially lead or exhaust fumes, is energy-depleting. Where resistance is substantially lowered, by environmental factors, this adds to the severity of any internal psychological problem and the length of treatment needed. Diet is another factor which may relate to either allergic problems or poor nutrition. An inadequate, unbalanced diet, deficient in essential elements, especially minerals and vitamins, de-natured by commercial storage, preparation and instant cooking (micro-wave) gives a diet which is filling, but one which fails to give the best stimulus to the physical and psychological needs of the individual. In this way fast food and the quick snack, cause tension and fear especially when taken with a caffeine-loaded beverage.

Other externals causing fear, are job insecurity or dissatisfaction, threats of redundancy or a prolonged industrial action. Working long hours, without a break in an over-crowded, open-plan office, lacking ventilation or natural daylight also creates a physiological imbalance marked by anxiety and fear. In some cases such imbalance may take the form of a violent over-reaction to others.

Alcohol alters the experience of self and others when in excess, because it is a toxic substance. Reactions of depression, fear, confusion and personality change occur from altered organ and nervous-system functioning. Synthetic pharmaceutical drugs, of the tranquillizer and anti-depressant type, can also create the conditions they seek to cure or alleviate. The side effects of the remedy may aggravate an existing problem, or create new psychological symptoms, as tension or panic, which add further to confusion, fear or uncertainty.

Internal Factors

These are the common emotional causes which differ for each individual, because of genetic factors, sensitivity and temperament, environment as well as previous hurts and trauma. The experience of rejection, pain or disappointment can cause insecurities which last a lifetime. Other problems as jealousy, envy, excessive rivalry, resentment, greed, and frustration, also cause insecurity, anxiety or fear, when there is sensitivity and repeated pressures. Similarly any sudden loss or change may be a threat to security, putting psychological health to the test especially where need and vulnerability are exposed.

Neurosis and Fear

Neurotic fear is always inappropriate, and an excessive emotional reaction to an external situation, distorted into a replica of an earlier one. Neurotic fear is seeing the present 'now' in terms of a past 'then', with a misguided logic which seeks to repeat and reassure as well as to annihilate. There is psychological blockage, with failure of development in the present, so that inevitably relationships are blocked, narrowed and distorted, provoking fear, doubt and mistrust. The neurotic gains of such situations are those of control and a re-stating or re-confirmation of unconscious certainties however limiting, and a reason for distress and anguish over the years.

The Manifestations of Neurotic Fear

At times indistinguishable from healthy reactions of intuition and sensitivity, there is often apprehension or tension with a sense of oppression, pressure, tremor and the inability to relax. Fear causes a sense of emptiness, having no stuffing, no inside, causing a feeling of vacuum. Isolation and loneliness are part of the cutting-off process. Palpitations, pain, fainting, exhaustion, diarrhoea, vomiting and nausea reflect the physiological over-activity due to psychological tension and imbalance. Fear can undermine every physiological activity – even sleep and relaxation in a familiar situation because every thought is dictated by a known past – or an anxious future.

Fear and Phobias

Agoraphobia concentrates psychological threats and dangers into more localised, symbolic areas of space and travel, especially the inability to move freely in public places and exposed open spaces where there are people or traffic. The phobia is a block to momentum, movement and escape. Because of the constant threats of collapse, or a panic attack, they cling to edges, unencumbered spaces near to home and safe; familiar relationships and situations, keeping new contacts minimal. Claustrophobia is a similar related problem with an immuring or locking-away of personal identity. The real self is enclosed by areas of overwhelming fear and insecurity, creating a dread of every new situation where there is no easy exit. Buses, lifts, trains and crowds are the common phobic situations, which dominate the whole of life. The fear of being trapped, symbolises the essential problem of a personal identity being locked away without outlet, exit or expression.

Fear and Inferiority

Inferiority feelings are closely related problems, rooted in comparison, competition and fear. There are often strongly, unexpressed ambivalent feelings towards someone close who in phantasy is punished or made to feel small. Identification results in the feelings of insignificance. Size, appearance, success, possessions and status are all over-valued. The overwhelming anger and resentment is infantile in origin with outburst of child-like rage. Often the origins have been lost, and past links and associations which limit growth and personal expression are no longer recalled. The wish is to feel superior, unassailable, without vulnerability or weakness. Inferiority feelings are replaced by secret phantasies of enhanced status, being in charge, or superior to others, which does little to build real security. The combination of outer, conscious inferiority feelings and internal pressures with secret, omnipotent phantasy demands keeps the neurotic process alive and more difficult to resolve. For long periods reality and original, creative ideas are minimal limited by the anxiety-assumptions.

Fears and Anxiety

Anxiety is fear where there is an excess of guilt and tension. Limitation, pressure, caution and anticipation are also associated, because of threats, supposedly external in origin, but really coming from a highly distorted reality. The true emotional facts and causes are kept carefully hidden, denied, suppressed and buried in a ball of pent-up knots of feelings, usually centred in the pit of the stomach, chest or throat. The worst attacks are triggered off by unexpected or unprepared for contacts, creating a complex of barely controlled feelings and impulses. Fear, rage, terror and tears are all over-reactions to the situation because of weakened controls. Much of the anxiety floods upwards in strong emotional currents. At the same time there is a dread of them becoming recognized or known to others. There is a constant need to push everything down – opinions as well as personality, in case feelings cannot be contained or get 'out of hand'. The constant upsurge of a need for expression combined with the neurotic control drains energy to such an extent that it provokes collapse, panic or breakdown. Like the genie of the lamp, the 'demon' feelings and impulses must be contained and bottled-up – pushed down in case they take over.

Fears and Phobic Problems

Whenever a phobic problem occurs, there is always a strong psychological association to the specific object or situation which pin-points the particular area of fear and dread. The phobic area is always symbolic although seemingly illogical. It nevertheless is an area of considerable emotional force influencing the whole life-pattern of the person, and often those around them. There may be the common phobia of insects, rodents, heights, flying or death, or more unusual ones. Some phobias are passed to a sensitive child by other members of the family. Sometimes the fear of dentists, thunder or mice perpetuates these within the susceptible mind of a child or adult. Energy responses of rage and anger are controlled and checked at every point by an elaborate system of taboos and superstitions – in case they get out of hand or overwhelm in some way.

Exercises to Reduce Fear

1 Clarify as far as possible the root-causes of a
particular fear area. Define carefully when
and where they occur and any known factors
that trigger or aggravate them. Almost
certainly the problem has an infantile
origin, expressed by immature attitudes in
adult areas. Make such causes clear by
thinking back to any significant times in
childhood when fear was induced or made
predominant. Get any known causes clear
and leave the 'unknown', unconscious ones,
for later insight work, as is possible. Ask
others in the family what they think and if
they can help to clarify the root origins.
When phobias have been present since
birth, there may have been a major
disturbance or trauma during pregnancy or
at the time of the actual birth – either
physical or psychological in nature.

2 **Clarify Negative-Certainty Thoughts
and their Effects**

This means not only the logical, conscious
understanding of negative conviction, but
also clarifying it within yourself at a more
sensitivity-feeling level. Clarity is essential
to see just how these thoughts work, and

how they express themselves against you –
limiting growth movement and spontaneity.
Convictions are like horror stories, which
limit every new or potential situation for
change.

3 Clarify any Specific Thought Factors influencing Negative Certainty

As always, note these down as soon as they
are seen clearly. Your own negative
thoughts differ from other people's, because
they were created by you specifically to
control certain areas of relationship, closeness, energy and drive. Typical examples
are: – I feel afraid –, I am worried about –, I
dread the worst happening –, It's terrifying
–, I fear that –, I fear dying –, I think I have
a disease –, I am incurable, It will happen –,
I know it will –, I can't forget, – I am no
good. Define the areas most feared, how
these inhibit and limit you as a result.
Where a specific figure is involved, try to
clarify how this fits into other patterns.
Sibling rivalry or problems with parental
figures, where a fear situation is created,
may be a re-creation of the family triangle.
Note the basic, unadmitted aim, of limiting
you now, not then, nor in the future, but
always in the evolving now.

4   Next define your positive areas of limited or minimal threat, – where you feel relatively safe. There may be no fears present with younger children, or adults may dispel fear because they create security. In others it is the elderly who give serenity and safety. Fear of trains, of flying, going out, or being in public is usually related to a fear of not being able to squeeze yourself back into the same old narrow perspectives after exposure to a new and exciting, stimulating situation. Define the boundaries and limits carefully of your fear. Draw or shape them if it helps make them clearer, or use any art form to express them and gain greater clarity and insight.

Where there is a specific fear, as of insects, mice, snakes, spiders, bridges or heights, try to get the motivations and boundaries clear. Clarify each situation of threat, whether worse with or without people, the time of day, sometimes the seasons. All may play a part and help you get closer to the real reasons and a true understanding. Try to see each fear symptom as symbolic only of your internal drives and wishes. Pay most attention to their actions and effect on you and others. You may get clues to meanings from dreams which reflect the same prevailing theme, and only use a different metaphor to protect sleep. Odd, overlooked, forgotten associations may also give clues. Don't be afraid to see how fear is limiting and controlling you.

However severe the problem, there are always certain people with whom you will feel more at ease. Whenever possible be with people who relax and make you feel peaceful rather than those who create tension. Talk with them and discuss openly your symptoms if it seems relevant, helpful and of interest.

5 Start to find areas of overlap, situations of confidence and fear where there is a mixture of both. Look carefully for these, if necessary take time to clarify them over a period of weeks. As a fear problem has usually been with you for a long time, you can also allow yourself lots of time to resolve it. Don't rush yourself into a pressure situation as you work at a problem. Begin slowly, in areas where there is withdrawal or avoidance, but some confidence too. Look closely at the realities, the true reasons for withdrawal and see where to begin to change them. Watch progress and keep records. Notes taken give positive feedback and you may need to refer and add to them later. On a 'good' day, when more relaxed or confident, do more. On a bad, or 'off' day, do less, but start somewhere, reducing your fear areas by confronting them and replacing them more by a reality approach. Aim to do some work every day at your own pace, even if just briefly. See this as your personal challenge and area of action for growth and resolution of some the limiting factors to you as a more extended human being.

6 Talk to people and discuss *their* limitations caused by fear. Tell them how you are positively tackling the problem and initiatives taken. In an actual fear situation talk to others, don't stay silent or hide and run. Don't keep fears or their resolution secret. If there is no one to talk to, write to someone about them, if necessary an article or letter to a newspaper, magazine or local radio. But find someone who is sympathetic and willing to listen, but you also must *be* sympathetic and a good listener yourself. Make the effort. There is much to be gained by making such contacts, and each one may help unravel a problem area. Turn fears into more ordinary conversation, reducing their omnipotence and power. In general talk, listen, share, and be as open as possible.

7 Clarify how fear inhibits and limits, and what aspect of your abilities and potentials are at this moment being reduced as a result. Understand the meaning, function and logic behind the thoughts of fear. They have their reasons, directions and aims, however much the actual panic situation seems senseless and meaningless. Fear is based on phantasy expectation rather than reality perception and reality factors. It relates to fixation, clinging to a known familiar past, rather than a changing present, and often the refusal to accept it causes the apprehension, vulnerability and weakness.

8 Start specific positive counter-suggestions to balance negative certainty and imagery. Positive thought affirmation should be repeated daily, as a specific opposite to negative certainty. When combined with visualisation, this creates a positive framework, an optimum for growth and limitation of fear. Visualise a specific problem clearly in your mind as you make the affirmation and see yourself clearly overcoming it.

9 Be Positive about Fear and use fear creatively.

a Write a letter or article to a friend, magazine or newspaper about how fear undermines, and how it can be resolved creatively.

b Start a local fear group, to support and inform others with similar problems. Provide a support for them and a forum of discussion for growth.

c Write a poem or a children's story about how fear was overcome.

d Paint or weave a picture showing the same theme and its resolution.

e Photograph freedom from fear in as many different situations as you are can perceive it. Show, and discuss the photographs with others.

f   Write down other examples where fears were overcome and put the ideas into action.The examples may be historical.

Let your fear-energy work *for* you, not against you. In this way it will become part of your totality rather than an undermining fragment of it. Don't stay in isolation. Make fear earn its keep. Work-out and create new, even better, alternatives than the six examples above. Put at least some into practice including your own. Especially be more out-going towards others with similar problems. Think positively about others as you work to resolve your own fear areas, not only about yourself, and your own problems and needs.

More General Points on Reducing Fear

1 Accept change with an open mind, as something new and exciting. Don't run away from it because it is new. You will be running away from life itself and nothing can replace that. The experience of difference is the experience of life, as it unfolds, expands, and re-shapes in a wide variety of unexpected forms and changing expressions.

2 When you are on display or in the limelight, you do not have to show the whole of you, only what is relevant to to the task in hand. Accept every occasion, however new or unfamiliar, as an invitation to self-expression, meeting every situation as creatively as possible. Always get on and do your best, without thinking too much or analysing intellectually. The best way to overcome fear in a display or public situation is to start to become more involved with your own particular task or role. If you are performing, accept anxiety or tension as normal and don't panic, become overwhelmed or 'thrown' by it. In such situations it is important to do your best and to build on every occasion, as it is accomplished and completed.

Building-up and developing self-appreciation, neutralises tendencies to self-depreciation. A good performance at the time helps to limit self-negatives afterwards. Never turn down or refuse an invitation and use it positively to overcome fear. Whatever your gifts and abilities, be positive, with style, and confidence. Don't deny or hide interests and talents, as their expression leads to growth and experience which helps to lessen fear and any lack of confidence.

After a pressure or public 'event' is over, relax and unwind. Stagefright and tension fade rapidly after the event and usually during the performance, once started. Even if you think that your showing was not particularly good, or even bad, stay involved with others afterwards to counter-balance negative self-imagery. Feedback from others helps diminish any tendency to judge yourself. What matters is the overall experience rather than any one aspect or part taken in isolation.

Deal with anticipatory fears well beforehand by relaxation and a holding back of too much excitement, apprehension or pre-judgement. Just relax quietly, stay you and don't think too much. Limit surges of feeling, judgement or tension beforehand, however pleasurable. Try generally to be less self-critical, more caring and involved with the feelings and needs of others. Conserve energy more by a 'win or lose' attitude. Do your best on a particular day, you cannot do more and that is enough. You are not a saint or a martyr, or fighting battles. Just be and express yourself. Be more easy and tolerant with others, as well as with yourself and once the expectations and intolerances have lessened, so too will the fear.

It is only rarely helpful to hold 'post mortems' after the event, they usually serve to intensify misery and negative certainty. Accept success or failure as part of the totality of each experience, the need to grow and to learn. Keep in touch with feelings at all times especially any dominating ones. It is much more positive and healthy to be in touch and aware of the present, the emerging new, rather than thinking too much about the past or the future.

On the Problem of Chronicity

Fear is always based on assumption and phantasy when it is neurotic in type. We are not here concerned with a healthy response to danger situations which is part of judgement and self-preservation. Chronic fear problems create chronic threats, limiting self-expression, personality growth and experience. Distortion at any level creates problems which block healthy development. Every chronic problem can be resolved as can an acute one, given healthy attitudes. There is usually internal resistance and argument against initiating any new involvements or new moves, but such changes are vital. A change and shift in attitudes is essential to reduce chronic problems. Remember – the first step is always the longest.

See problems of chronic fear as active fragments and remnants of a hurtful, painful past rather than relating to the present. Defensive negative attitudes are counter-arguments to closeness, new contacts, exploration and new expressions, aiming to limit and counteract every encounter or experience of life.

All neurotic fear, and all neurosis, is an attempt to revive and recreate a previous pattern in the present. Inevitably, neurotic insistence ends with frustration and disappointment, whatever the apparent gains in the control and manipulation of others. It can be transformed by a determined creative move, once initiated and admitted. All attempts to artificially control reality with a contrived present end in disappointment. Yet all neurosis seeks to do this, to control life and others by 'bogey' motives of self-defeating fear. No one can stop the lifeflow or live in the past. The neurotic position stimulates anxiety by its prejudgements, importing danger, phantasy and uncertainty into the unfolding present. As the personal self is drawn into a complicated spiral of emotion, real caring and true self expression is lost, which is the reason for the loneliness and depression which are so often present.

As far as possible, limit motives of self-interest and self-protection. Self-orientated attitudes ultimately drain psychological strength and nourishment because they are not outwards-directed. Support and develop interest in the present, especially new areas that expand you more. A new, creative interest is not usually part of a neurotic web. Exploring and initiating fosters new contacts, new perceptions, with feed-back and a reality which you can build on. Once infantile assumptions are less dominant or intrusive, fear can be integrated into a psychological totality, part of an overall internal mosaic rather than a fragment acting in isolation and self-interest.

Chapter five

On Relationships, Making Friends and Meeting People

The making and development of relationships at multi-levels is fundamental for everyone because of the contact, stimulation and information they provide. Relationships are essential for health and survival in a modern world. The ability to relate, give-out, respond and listen to others gives a satisfying as well as essential psychological contact, and new reality boundaries that help combat phantasy assumptions and to differentiate them from reality. The depth of a relationship and degree of closeness can be greatly facilitated by language, areas of common interest, culture and social background, but non-verbal elements also play a major role, such as eye-contact, smiling, gesture, touching, holding and spontaneity in general.

The supply of adequate food, shelter, work and security depends on an ability to communicate freely and to make meaningful relationships. Apart from the basic survival needs, the psychological ones of affection, sharing, trust and closeness are just as dependent upon healthy open communications for their expression and continuation.

Healthy Attitudes towards the Self

Where these are at all confined, limited, over-defended or distorted, the basic picture of the self becomes limited and one-sided giving a false image of self and others. Every meeting and contact can be interpreted through a distorted viewpoint of the world, and others seen from one particular frame of imagery and not in an overall balanced totality. Because of distortion, the quality of life and closeness becomes out of true. With more healthy self-imagery, and self-acceptance, there can be more openness, confidence and trust. The acceptance of frailty and imperfection of oneself, as well as the weaknesses and faults of others, leads to a much healthier psychological position.

Healthy Attitudes towards Others

Basic to more balanced relationships is seeing and perceiving others as they are and not according to your phantasy fears or assumptions. It is vital to sense and respond to people as they are actually without altering their reality to our own internal world. It is important not to see others from the peaks of narcissism or neurosis but as they are when we experience them. In this way interest, closeness, understanding and giving can develop and grow rather than be used as attempts to reinforce and confirm old patterns and assumptions. We are all inter-dependent and need others for survival – physically as well as psychologically. Giving-out attitudes stimulate positive responses essential to health and growth. Relationships help free us from past hurts and phantasy-expectations and to be more ourselves in the present rather than re-enacting a role from the past. Such contacts are needed consistently in order to be more open and in contact with the present, otherwise there is a risk of being psychologically impoverished.

Learning from Others

All learning comes ultimately from within and being psychologically prepared for change. The maturing self learns from each experience, whether good or bad, giving an orientation which develops understanding. Learning occurs physically as well as intellectually and psychologically, acquiring new attitudes, skills and perceptions, as long as there are flexible attitudes which permit change to occur. Openness of attitude and communication are essential for learning to take place and the appreciation of others. Giving-out or giving-back, stimulates and extends by broadening areas of experience, interest and knowledge.

Laughing with Others

The sharing of humour, laughter, and letting-go in general, supports more balanced perspectives. Laughter has always been one of our best medicines, and the unexpected twists of meaning, context and association which catch us off guard, help break through routine attitudes and soften more rigid ones. This sudden letting-go, however temporary, gives a better balance at quite deep psychological levels, a brief moment of insight into our certainties and too confident predictions of outcome – which the joke proves wrong.

Humour turns the tables, not just on the listener, but on his defences. Taking anything too seriously, is rarely positive and the lack of consideration of alternatives creates an unhealthy, set attitude. A healthy allowance for the vicissitudes of human nature as well as life's uncertainties, gives a better balance and a sense of humour. When too much is demanded from the self, then less than perfect cannot be tolerated in others. Humour gives a better balance and a more overall perspective, to help overcome rigid attitudes.

Listening to Others

The key to understanding and relating, is to listen more – physically, with the outer ear as well as internally with the psychological one. The inner intuitive ear helps correct the external impressions and corrects what is seen as only factual. Listening means understanding the themes, feelings and expressions of others, without interruption or comment at the time. It should be an active process, one dynamic and attentive but not contrived at or forced. When complete, there is listening with the inner intuitive ear, hearing not just the spoken word, but also what is unsaid. In this way there is no loss of contact or split between functioning, feelings, and reactions and the unspoken, non-verbal, inner dimensions which direct the choice of verbal phrase.

Giving and Sharing with Others

Giving is basic to receiving, and for all true psychological growth. We build-up, develop and grow internally by a combination of experience, identification, and contact, with figures in our environment. Where these are absent, or neglected because of non-giving attitudes one also feel deprived and unloved. When others are cared for generously by a giving-out of self, this leads to feelings of being cared for and enriched. Only the act of giving to another, whatever the situation or pressures, leads to a sense of real love and caring.

At some time everyone experiences pain, rejection or refusal. Rejection hurts because of hurt pride and the rage it engenders, but indifference is worse and the most harmful experience of all.

Spontaneity

It is generally better to say what you think at the time rather than to bottle-it-up with regret later. Every feeling, positive or negative, must have a life, an outlet or expression, even if wrong and later regretted. A crippled personality or psychosomatic illness may be the outcome of blocked feelings, permanently limiting personality growth. In general say what you think but apologise later when you were in the wrong.

Having Friends is Being One First

Friendship is primarily interest, liking and caring for another with acceptance of different and other points of view and being able to disagree. Appreciating the other as a unique person is the essence of friendship. It also implies being able to differ and to disagree about ideas and opinions and not having to impose a viewpoint. Friendship first and foremost tolerates difference. Sympathetic understanding leaves you free to choose, to stay different and distinct if you want to, without loss of caring, affection or loss of status. This sense of basic acceptance by another as a distinct, individual human being, is the essence of friendship.

Shedding, Forgetting and Forgiving

Mental elimination is as vital as bowel elimination. It is just as important to forget as to remember and recall. The inability to let go of past hurts and traumas, leading to repetitive preoccupations, is negative and damaging, undermining relationships and understanding, also preventing growth. Maturity and hindsight often combine to give wisdom that support forgiveness and forgetting, a shedding of past hurts which would otherwise stay within the psychological tissues as an irritant. Any retention of old negatives creates bitterness, resentment and hate, undermining love and trust. Feelings of revenge or rejection take over the personality and lead to alienation and depression.

The Art of Conversation

There is no secret about making conversation, it is the spontaneous putting into words of thoughts and ideas as they occur, in a way that is both natural and sensitive to the needs and feelings of the other. Conversation is affected by situation, prevailing mood and any social cultural pressures of the time. It is the verbal expression of ideas and feelings and a response to the particular contact, situation and feelings stimulated by others. It is always strongly influenced by both mood and confidence.

For good conversation to occur there must be: -

1   Attentive listening, interest and sensitivity to the other person's point of view and individuality.

2   A relaxed confident state of mind, not unduly anxious or depressed.

3   A giving-out and letting go of ideas, and spontaneous sharing without pre-judgement, fear or certainty.

4   The willingness and confidence to verbalise and to communicate feelings in words as a way of expressing feelings.

5   An acknowledgement of the listener as a person and an appreciation of his or her thoughts, ideas and opinions.

6   Being prepared to contact, learn and grow, to extend habitual concepts and ideas. In this sense all conversation is a growth because it gives the opportunity for new perspectives, sharing, interchange and learning to develop.

7   Basic trust must be present for conversation to take place, with sufficient security to allow for a spontaneity of ideas and feelings to emerge and give shape and form to words.

8 Conversation is a verbal relationship which has sufficient relaxation and psychological space for a creative interchange to occur. In this way ideas expressed have sufficient depth and individuality for mutual interest and personal expression.

9 Conversation always means time for listening to others as well as talk, with sensitivity to the the underlying feelings and needs which the words inevitably trigger. In this way it links up the overall totality of the persons involved.

10 Conversation is sharing. Words and ideas may be the basic bricks of conversation, but ultimately all conversation is about feeling, relationships, sharing and contact.

Public Speaking

Speaking before an audience, either a formal address or an informal after-dinner speech, is always an exposure, an open sharing of the self to some degree. On each occasion there is a relationship to a group or collective situation rather than a one-to-one or a few, as in conversation. If there is too much insecurity, an audience can be turned into an ordeal or threat. Where the audience is seen more as a global whole, rather than a mass of minds and people, it is quite possible to feel at ease and relaxed.

Practise as often as you can in public situations, at every level. Never turn down an occasion to talk in public or to a group. Until you are confident, be well prepared beforehand, but in an informal situation, try talking 'off the cuff'. Dont be frightened to talk from notes, but make these less detailed with mainly headings and pointers. Feel more of an authority in the areas you know about, and don't deny your own experiences and knowledge. Give the audience what they want at their level, as long as it also includes what you want to say.

'Difficult' People

In reality there are no difficult people – only those who do not conform to our expectations, attitudes and patterns. They are as 'difficult' as we make them so or because of attitudes and defences which demand and expect others to be or to conform to predicted norms and boundaries. They often pose a threat or challenge to established thinking – opinions and attitudes, carefully erected over the years. Looking for familiar attitudes to confirm established viewpoints is aimed at personal comfort only, rather than growth or change. 'Difficult' people are also positive people, because they offer a challenge, a potential re-thinking of attitudes, viewpoints and opinions, taken for granted. It is not uncommon later to establish firm friendships, because 'difficult' people are needed as much as different people. We develop a respect and liking for those able to differ, and to confront, question or challenge our cherished opinions. Differences of opinion allow us to see ourselves better and make us re-think our positions.

Every challenge, whatever its source, is important provided it is not consistently negative and undermining. The systematic psychological flattening of another human being cannot lead to sharing or closeness. A positive difference is often welcome, despite some initial antagonism to challenge of a position held. Where there is rigidity, another viewpoint helps emotional balance, and to fully appreciate the alternatives. You don't have to agree with different ideas but you should look and consider them.

Don't disagree either just because an opinion is different. The 'difficult' response is a challenging one that may clarify your position. Don't be afraid to agree if you think the other person is right, but never take a passive, self-negating attitude for the sake of peace and to placate. When you don't agree, say so firmly in a balanced way and say where you disagree. Aim to stay yourself as you listen and consider, keeping emotional reactions minimal rather than dominating. Differences are inevitable because people are different and their viewpoints reflect this. Because of growth, evolution and change, everyone needs to listen and to regularly re-assess their viewpoints and perceptions. As we mature, we develop new depths and we broader perspectives and we are more able to accept change however certain and firm the earlier convictions.

Barriers to Relationships

Barriers to a relationship are usually negative, unless the relationship itself is destructive, when a barrier is essential for self-protection and survival.

A patient seen recently with Multiple Sclerosis was tired with no reserves, just able to function without collapse. She was being propositioned by a young man who insisted on ringing, and trying to see her all the time. She was not in love with him and his attentions were unwelcome and unrealistic. Most of all they drained her. It was essential for her continued survival that she erect a barrier to his calls and attempts to see her. With few exceptions, every relationship is an encounter and has some potential for learning and a positive experience which can help re-think existing attitudes. The calling into question of an opinion or attitude may provoke defensiveness and resentment because all change is seen as a threat to security and a known position.

Anger and Violence

This is often the expression of weakness, poor controls and insecurity. There is intolerance of anything new or different, and a more familiar situation is preferred to one where real changes are called for. Violence changes the rules, threatening a psychological challenge by a physical one. In this way it ignores the real problems and what they represent. The expression of anger often gives relief from tension and a feeling of breakthrough – like tears, only more intense. Violent rage is negative and destructive unless contained and talked about. Sometime an outburst of rage is needed to break through an intolerable situation, after years of denial or suppression. Violence nearly always leaves the underlying problems unresolved, and has nothing to recommend it. Spontaneous anger is healthy, but suppressed diverted anger leads only to further frustration or violence, neither of which is positive or psychologically healthy.

Avoidance

Fear of looking at a new situation or a challenging one is often because of fear of facing up to the self. There is dislike of change in any form, having to reconsider a new position, priority or aim. Past mistakes, may also be painful, when linked to pride and certainty. Where the outcome of change or challenge is a threat of humiliation or deflated pride, this also leads to avoidance, or to blinkered attitudes of shame and guilt.

Prejudice

Prejudice is any fixed judgemental attitude of certainty, usually opposed to modification or change. There may be quite hard, unbending attitudes towards others, with a limited flexibility of caring and giving. Prejudice is negative because it is limiting and and refuses to admit reasonable alternatives. Because it pre-judges others, it also pre-judges the self and in this way it limits moves towards others as well as contact with them.

Negative Attitudes as a Barrier to Relationships

1 Jealousy

This is a barrier to relationships because of a preoccupation with another or third person, felt to deprive, limit or take away. They are felt to rob them of something or someone – which is their possesion. In this way they are felt to have taken an unfair advantage. There may be jealousy of another man or woman, their position, ability or looks. Excessive preoccupation and suspicion deprives them of vitality and energy, and further convinces them that they are wrongly deprived. Lack of confidence by over-valuing others adds to feelings of misery, rage and unhappiness, as well as self-dislike and isolation.

2 Possessiveness

This is similar to jealousy and may anticipate it. There is an over-emphasis on things, objects and possessing – the externals and tangibles of a relationship. The basic reason is a constant need for proof of being lovable, from lack of a confident sense of existing, which constantly alienates them from a secure identity. Neither things nor people are really valued however, other than for the reassurance and temporary security they bring. Because possessiveness is also narcissistic, it is self-orientated and can never achieve what it seeks – a personal sense of worth and value. Ultimately this leads to depression and futility unless greater giving-out and caring can be found.

3 Envy

Here there is a negative comparison of self and others with destructive phantasies. The term 'eaten-up' with envy gives a clue to the degree of primitive destructive feelings, associated with the supposed better fortunes of others. The phantasies are attached to a sense of personal failure or inadequacy – often the direct outcome of the paralysis which envy engenders. The gap between self and others is felt to be large because envy-phantasies drain self-esteem rather than adding to it. A great deal of primitive phantasy centres around envy problems, the fear of damaging others or being damaged by them, all of which diminishes confidence and distorts reality.

Exercises in Relationships and Making Friends

The Cure

1 Start by clarifying the real friends you have. Almost certainly there is someone you like, or wish to know more, who you can talk with, and share ideas and feelings. Develop this relationship by giving more to it, especially more of yourself. Try to widen its scope by including other people who you know less well but whose company you enjoy.

2 The best friends are often those you have known the longest, even if you have lost contact with them. Begin here too, and if a contact has been lost, write or telephone. Make a new contact or link again. The gap in time usually makes little difference to old friends, and true friends are always pleased to hear from you. Develop these friendships because of their roots, as you develop other new friends and interests.

3 Try more honestly to see the role you play in the lack of friendships – what it is you do, and how you put others off. Are you giving-out enough to them? Are you interested

enough? Do you have a problem with certain age-groups – your own sex or the opposite? Spend time to see how, where and why you are erecting blocks, then work out how to alter them. If necessary see the solution for others with a similar problem first before you define it for yourself.

4   See more clearly where to make changes, particularly in attitudes towards others. Also, if you have changed in any way over the years, in openness and spontaneity, the sort of 'vibes' or signals you give out to others. Are you still being influenced by the past in the way you look, receive and perceive others? Do you still see them through childhood, adolescent, even parental eyes? Was there a hurt in childhood, after a loss which significantly changed and embittered you? If there has been this sort of change, are you now too defended? Try to see what you unconsciously hope to gain. Ask others how they see you. If necessary write down your own impressions of how you think they see you, for enhanced insight and self-knowledge.

5   Every friendship must be based on a giving-out of self with a sharing of interest and sympathy as well as of listening. Note how much you are giving out of the real you. Clarify major areas of interest, which you like and, where you are most interested and

enthusiastic. These are the areas where you are more likely to be able to give to others, to infuse them with some of your drive.

6　Having clarified the major areas of concern, aim to contact, support and work with others in your community with similar interests. This usually involves help in a local group situation, perhaps help with a local charity, but it will also support friendships and relationships. Get information about suitable groups from your library, support them positively and contribute. If you cannot be active, involved regularly, go whenever you can. But listen and give as much time and help as possible. Encourage others, contribute, and be as interested as possible.

7　If there is not a local group that covers your sphere of interest, then start one yourself. If you feel already over-involved with people, saturated, needing to be alone, seeing people all the time but never able to get near, look closely again at your attitudes, to see where you invite non-involvement and defensiveness. Work out your own exercises and solutions making these as specific as possible.

If you have an obsessional-phobic pattern of thinking, so that every meeting – real or anticipated, is one of fear, then clarify your particular negative assumptions as soon as possible. Try to see which feelings of jealousy, envy, shock or anger precede an obsessional problem and make it more entrenched. Enlarge and develop any specific areas of limitation. Define where you put up barriers and relate a specific problem to the specific chapter which deals with it. Be a lot more honest and open with yourself as you define self-limiting boundaries. Aim always to see why. See where and how you are putting up barriers, and in what situations. Try to see the gains and logic behind them. Write notes on these areas but don't become excessive, literary, or obsessional about them. One or two sheets of paper should be sufficient to note the salient points for each area as a basis for fuller self-work and understanding.

8 If you have no interests, no friends, not even former ones, and you cannot relate to others at all, never could for as long as you can recall, then begin now. It is never too late, and it is only as difficult as you yourself make it, not more so. If you basically like people and want to get closer to them, to have friends, then become one first to someone who needs you without trying to analyse how and why it can happen. If this makes no sense, seems too difficult or impossible, ask your local library for a social contact group or association for others who are lonely and isolated in your area. Begin

somewhere and begin now. Start in a small way and begin by giving out more with a friendly helping hand to others in need. Consider others more than your own needs.

9 Finally if you feel that you really don't like people at all, don't want to know them, that you prefer animals to humans, your own company or solitude to others, then try to contact others who feel the same way. Try to make a contact with someone who shares your present viewpoints, even your beliefs or prejudices, but find someone who will listen and share as well as just talk.

10 Write down your own exercise here.

Chapter six

Shyness

Shyness is always a block to individuality, creative expression and development, however much it seems part of the natural outcome of a sensitive temperament. Being shy and over-sensitive is inevitably limiting because it sees the opinions and viewpoints of others as either more successful or critical, often both, and any personal contribution as shameful or in-adequate. Other people are seen rigidly, as a threat rather than as individuals. Because of the passivity and withdrawal, the shy person tends to be generally over-dependent on others rather than inter-dependent with them. Shy-ness distorts, leading to vulnerability and weakness. Over-sensitivity comes from ex-cessive idealistic attitudes of perfection, but too often ideals of others rather than a reasonable and accurate assessement of the self.

Associated Mental Attitudes

Attitudes of passivity, masochism, anxiety or self-consciousness with others expresses suppressed drives and aggression, reflected back upon the self, causing guilt or shame feelings. The typical withdrawal is based on expectation of criticism, failure and low self-esteem, with insecurity which adds to self-consciousness. This is excessive, painful and self-generated, differing from healthy awareness because of the projection into others of aggression and sexuality which drives deep holes into confidence and identity.

Insecurity Adding to Weakness and Vulnerability

In most shy people, psychological development and maturity lag behind physical and intellectual attainment because of anxiety, the dread of exposure or 'making a mess'. There is a lack of fulfilling psychological contacts and natural expressions which would create more ease and a greater sense of belonging and comfort.

Showing-off to Get Attention

Shy people tend to compensate for shyness by seeking approval – to be seen, noticed and accepted. Trying to be both in the limelight and in the wings at the same time, creates discomfort and dis-ease which is not always easy to understand at the time. Over-valuing others with the need to have their love and approval creates much of the embarrassment and tension in social situations, although this is quite unconscious. The shy person feels in a situation of exposure, however much they cling to the periphery, became of overwhelming drives to be seen, noticed, and approved of.

The Attractive Side of Shyness

Shyness has also a certain naturalness about it. In general, this comes from the over-sensitivity and vulnerability, often with a seductive, sexual aspect to a communication. Shyness is the expression of non-verbal, unexpressed wishes and attitudes towards others, in addition to what is obvious and known about. The seductive attitudes are deeply unconscious so that the attention it attracts cannot be openly admitted. Some of the shame and guilt is the belief that such sexuality is wrong, bad or should be punished.

The Most Common Areas of Shyness

Shyness is always felt in the presence of others, though sometimes at the thought, of another, especially when meeting someone new or unfamiliar who is more easily represented as a threat to status or security. It is most common within the adolescent age group, especially with the opposite sex or someone 'parental', seen as superior because of the enormous drive and preoccupation at that time with sexuality, and status. This gives the clue to the amount of comparison and competition present. When combined with repression of sexuality the outcome is inner discomfort and discord.

Immaturity

Immaturity like shyness is centred around infantile attitudes and the powerful need to remain childlike towards others. It is the infantile nature of the sexuality, the impulses and needs which make them taboo and why the adolescent or adult feels uncomfortable and guilt-ridden. Infantile drives, expressed indirectly, tend to block more adult and mature drives and goals, creating confusion and often emotional chaos.

Over-Valuation of Others

This is always a problem in shyness, and linked as much to under-valuation of the self as to over-valuation of others. The expression of real positive appreciation and concern for others can be almost entirely lost by the self-negation and a sense of being worthless or a failure.

The Negative Side of Shyness

Shyness limits personal growth and the expression of healthy drives like aggression and sexuality. In this way, outward expansion is delayed or kept minimal. Because negative imagery puts barriers and limits on personal contact, there is always some stunting of experience and development.

Under-valuation of the Self

Under-valuation or devaluation of self is the outcome of over-valuation of others, acting as a constant stimulation to envy, competition, jealousy and rivalry. Sometimes disturbing infantile phantasies of revenge, power and control are stimulated which add to guilt, fear and shame. Under-valuation occurs because all others are made more lofty, beautiful, intelligent and successful, in this way on a pedestal and beyond attack. The few exceptions are both belittled and devalued.

A similar psychological mechanism occurs in the early stages of grief where blame and negation are turned upon the self for being negligent, the deeper feelings of anger at being left and abandoned are in this way kept hidden. The 'lost' person is protected from secret feelings of rage and resentment which would otherwise reverse the grief reaction.

A shy person feels undervalued, because he or she is too preoccupied with others, the over-involvement weakening identity, maturity and growth.

Narcissistic Aspects of Shyness

A great deal of the problem in shyness comes from an infantile need for reassurance which increases vulnerability as well as keeping all actual experiences limited and within narrow boundaries.

The Strength of Underlying Phantasies in Shyness

Because these are rooted in infancy, shyness phantasies are omnipotent, unreal, and repetitive. Underlying sexuality is infantile rather than adult and tends not to be matured by adult contacts because the involvement is such a shy partial one.

Guilt Feelings in Shyness

There is guilt because life is denied and passed by, not lived to the full. Contacts with others are both tenuous and fear-dominated. There is also guilt because of infantile omnipotent phantasies and their more secret gratifications, however hidden, vicarious and indirect.

The Influence and Role of the Family in Shyness

The family is important because of its tendency to encourage over-dependency. They may also need an outlet, someone to contain or to be a recipient of their collective guilt, including anger and repressed sexuality. The shy person is often a convenient psychological receptacle for such feelings. In many ways the shy person is a victim of the family system which colludes with and constantly reasserts the 'shy' position in many subtle ways. A family usually feels no guilt because outwardly it is helpful and sympathetic, but behind the scenes it is often over-protective and does little positive to enable the shy member to mature and develop independence.

The Need for Friends

Everyone needs friends. The shy person especially needs help from others who care, to gain a more balanced picture and perspective. They need to know how to relate to others, to protect themselves and to be more aware of the pressures and influences of others. In this way those who reinforce guilt, to keep them in an infantile, undeveloped position can be better confronted.

The Reason for Shyness

Shyness, however painful, has its reasons and its rewards. Much of the underlying motivation seeks to prevent indifference, criticism, anger or rejection because of infantile anxieties about loss of love. Nevertheless shyness also seeks to impose and to control by its very discomfort and embarrassment, whatever the cost to the person and the quality of their being.

New Situations, Difficult Moments, and How to Cope with Them

Difficult moments are essentially changing, and challenging ones, and an inseparable part of the emerging present not a phantasy picture of the past. Threats from a different situation, come only from within the self. A known actual situation is more easy to cope with than an anticipated one, but when the present is received and understood as it happens then fears, limitations and difficulties can be considerably reduced.

General Guidelines to the Resolution of Shyness

All neurosis is a product of negative certainty and negative specific thoughts which seek to perpetrate a known, usually infantile belief or attitude, and to fix this into each new experience in some way. However obvious, uncomfortable or shy you feel, try to talk and acknowledge shyness problems with less caring. Accept them as your limitation for the moment and be simple, natural and spontaneous about them when they occur. Listen more to others and take more interest in them – their drives, interest, goals and conversation. Listen, be concerned and ask questions. Become involved more to reduce the narcissism behind shyness.

In general, be less secretive, and more open. See your shyness as a surface, 'ego' thing, not related to your potential, identity or your inspirational depths.

Maximise contact with others and get used to being with them. Give-out more to others and be more honest with yourself, including your needs, aims, drives and sexuality. Be more accepting of yourself, less self-critical and analytical. Every drive and every phantasy, includes some aspect of your person and needs. No part of you should be either judged, elevated, or devalued – at least, not without careful thought and consideration.

Examples of the Specific Thought Convictions which Perpetuate Shyness

Typical examples are as follows, but always diagnose your own and write them down for clarity:-

1 I am inferior to others, less in some way

2 Others look at me, dislike or criticise me

3 They dislike me because I am shy and gauche, I look and feel awkward

4 Other people know or guess my thoughts

5 I am, and always will be shy, awkward, and embarrassed with others. Meeting strangers is a threat to me, because they criticise or dislike me

6 Other people make me feel awkward

7 I am not able to show feelings of anger, disagreement or to be assertive

8 I make a mess of things

9 Write your own example here of how you perpetuate shyness.

The Dynamics of Change

1   Clearly define your own negative thought attitudes which may or may not be included above.

2   Change the negatives to their opposite more positive affirmative quite consciously. Repeat them for as long as you persist with your shyness and negative self-attitudes. Repeat the positives until they are automatic, familiar and unconscious. Understand and recognise the specific motivations of your negations and how they are limiting. Assert – I am equal to others – when the thought-negative is – I am inferior, or less than others.

Do this consciously and let the positives become as much part of you as the negatives.

3   Avoid being secretive, and laid-back in your problem area. Be as open as you can with your problems, with yourself and with others.

4   Share, discuss and talk about yourself, your difficulties if others are interested, but don't bore them with constant talk of illness or problems. Although openness is not strictly necessary for cure, it is always supportive

whenever shyness is prevalent because of blocked, closed-in attitudes over the years.

5 Understand and see the specific thought-attitudes which create a problem. See how negative certainty and conviction bring negatives into reality.

6 See how negative certainty thoughts are a constant stimulus to shyness and discuss this aspect with a close friend or member of the family for greater clarification.

7 Acknowledge your needs openly – they are part of the essential you, and are not something to be ashamed of.

8 Also acknowledge needs to look and be looked at. Express these more openly without shame. Inversion of the need to look is a barrier in shyness with the sensation that everyone can either see or is looking at you.

9 Accept your body more openly and with less guilt – as something natural, but make it less emotionally dominated. Keep sexual overtures explicit, open, appropriate and 'honest'.

Develop spontaneity in your talking, laughing and thinking and have more fun, less shame, secrecy and guilt. Express yourself openly to diminish a hidden, denied you. This helps diminish limiting infantile fears. The more the self is hidden, the greater the phantasies, the denial and the distortion. As the true self gets pushed back from contacts with ease and openness in the background, so more limiting, indirect, emotional channels of expression, infantile supposition and demand develop. Such alternative exits provoke punishing fears, embarrassments and exaggerations which have no relevance to the present, to the you as you are in the present, here and now.

Listen more to others, trying to understand them, their needs, feelings, motivations and communications. Understand that others too have their insecurities, problems and needs just as you have.

Because shyness and blushing crush creative expression they turn life and others into an unreal threatening situation. Resolve to correct such distortions and misplaced personality patterns which limit, hurt, and distort you as well as others.

It is always painful to experience needs but when suppressed, they can become distorted into humiliating discomfort. For the shy person, feelings in general are on the surface, so that the least awareness, causes burning embarrassment as if suddenly exposed to the limelight.

Some degree of shyness is normal for everyone. In adolescents it is part of their overwhelming sexual feelings, at a time when psychological maturity is barely developed or is insufficient to contain them. They feel as if they will burst out, and overwhelm at any second, which adds to existing uncertainties. The need to attract and draw attention of the adolescent, contrasts with their strong needs to be adult, experienced, and more mature.

In middle age at the time of the menopause the same problems of blushing and bursts of heat recur, due to hormonal changes, but also because of a psychological re-awakening of adolescent needs, wishes and impulses at the same time.

Shyness in adults may sometimes be associated with a short-fuse and poor controls. Weakness of psychological defences leads to immaturity, especially where suppression of anger or strong feelings is a factor.

The shy person is often not weak but quite strong, seeking embarrassing attentions to act out infantile situations, leading to misunderstanding and confusion. Shyness can be an excuse to avoid, withdraw, or to forgo participation, but often there are equally strong needs for acceptance and involvement. The shy way of thinking and understanding distorts and moulds others into images which confirm and reinforce negative patterns, especially of shame and shyness.

The constant distortion of others is the obsessional thread to every shyness position and makes for much of its chronicity. It should be one of the earliest areas for work and correction. Some people are critical and disapproving, but rarely to the degree imagined. The kernel of shyness lies in a rigid supposition that others are threatening and criticising, at a time when they are not giving-out enough, in this way feeling more weak, vulnerable and open to criticism.

A traumatic background, with bad experiences – perhaps violence or rejection, worsens shyness, because it heightens and perpetuates aggression and resentment within immature channels. They are kept immature because they have insufficient adult expression and experience at a level which matters and can bring about growth or security. Shyness, secrecy and witholding add to immaturity, hence the need to be more open and for specific practise in spontaneity and sharing.

200

For these reasons, talk and express more of yourself as you are now – interests, needs and feelings. Do so in a relaxed, easy way, listening and interested in the needs and feelings of others. Don't expect your problem to be a major topic of social interest, or you will bore others and alienate yourself further. Talk spontaneously about common areas of interest and concern rather than your own problems and your pain. If you want to talk about shyness, be sure that it interests others and that it gives something to them as well. If not, such talking is self-defeating and a repeat of the narcissism which is the root-problem of all shyness.

Chapter seven

Emotional Tension

Tension exists when there is excess emotional energy within the physical channels of the body. Especially the muscles, ligaments and joints reflect the tension, which originates within the mind and the psychologicals. Tension is the product of an internal division, a wish or impulse to respond conflicting with one to withold, hold-back or retreat. The problem of a pressurised reality situation also causes tension. Usually this subsides once the problem has been resolved, unless there are physical or psychological reasons for its continuation.

Relative Frequency

Emotional tension is the commonest response to an emotional situation causing some degree of painful discomfort, often at both physical and cmotional levels. In every medical surgery, at least one problem in three is now directly related to psychological causes, or they are a factor somewhere in its causation.

Psychological Causes of Tension

Because of a conflict between spontaneous wishes to express, to be, and give out, with ambivalent opposing drives to withold, spontaneity is undermined. Feelings which belong to the present, especially the important ones of need, caring and love, are no longer spontaneous or natural, but more intense than reality would justify. The present is drowned in a sea of the feelings, doubts, fears and apprehension which swamp spontaneous expression, creative contact, relaxation and ease by unrecognizable anguish, spasm or pain.

Emotional Triggers

These vary with the individual, but where the mind is programmed to conflict and expectation of failure, almost any encounter or 'event' sets off a whole chain of negative thought processes and phantasies causing conflict and tension, wrong information and faulty perception. All of this puts extra pressure on the psychologicals sometimes to a degree that both physical functioning as well as the mental processes are extremely tense.

The Importance of Conscience

The healthy conscience reflects a positive, gentle, caring, aspect of man, neither critical, judgemental, disapproving nor moralising. In neurosis, rigid attitudes and excessive feelings makes the conscience tense, hard, unbending and intolerant in its attitudes so that judgements become fixed and inelastic, often punitive. Because of a lack of softness and gentleness, sensitivity is undermined and the interpretation and experience of the world is seen through hard lenses. Fixed, unyielding attitudes deviate the individual away from their original caring and spontaneity into rigid positions that stimulate and feed a judgemental conscience. Once hardened in this way, the conscience becomes the vehicle of gloom and doom, of fear, and self-hate, turning every situation into an encounter of tension and fear. The conscience is always made softer, and more human by forgiving, caring attitudes, which engender love, accepting and understanding.

The Feelings and Opinions of Others

When there is sensitivity and awareness, with understanding of others, then tension is lessened because there is less distortion of them into negative, threatening figures. Tension is always increased by negative expectation and knowing, aggravating every reality problem because it feeds primitive, usually aggressive phantasies into it.

On the Need to be Natural

It is essential to be natural at all times whatever the psychological or physical situation, even if this means a show of feelings, or losing control for a time. Until you can be yourself, centred and natural, you cannot fully perceive, understand and relate to others. Misunderstanding and misperception come from a confused position which inevitably causes relationship problems because of false imagery adding to existing tension.

The Damage of an Over-restrictive Upbringing

Parents and families often bear a heavy burden of responsibility for much of the neurosis in present-day society. Firmness is different from rigidity, and much of the past attitudes towards children has been too hard, unimaginative and unbending, or over flexible and pliable, so that the testing and exploring of boundaries, behaviour and attitudes was made more difficult. Restriction or suppression of individuality is never positive or desirable, and brings about resentment, anger, or tension because spontaneity of expression is blocked, and turned inwards, fearing an excessive or uncontrolled response.

Upbringing, and the Harm it can do

A rigid unbringing creates rigid people and rigid defences by processes of learning and identification. The defence against such damaging attitudes tends also to impose its own rules and limitations and these become a major contribution to tension and limitation. Parental attempts to force rigid patterns and ideas not in harmony with the child only create resentment and negative feelings, often impossible to express, causing life-long limitations to growth, health and spontaneity.

How Fear of Rejection Causes Tension

Anxiety about rejection can undermine every aspect of being, causing tension, misunderstanding and uncertainty. Fear feeds tension limiting ease and relaxation, so that physical pain, spasm, clumsiness or accident-proneness are common. Rejection is always a hurt because it is a threat to love. The pain which arises usually reflects a suppressed hostile response, and causing depression as there are no reasonable outlets for its expression.

Chronic Problems

Chronic problems often develop from unresolved acute areas, denied and ignored, or from a wrong approach and treatment to a problem area. Negative feelings fester and ferment when left to themselves in denial and isolation, blocking development, growth and experience. There is only limited psychological growth and an inability to be spontaneous. The sense of lack and feelings of resentment seems as if part of the self has been bitten-off, or kept alive vicariously, creating physical as well as psychological dis-ease.

Some More General Points

Balanced tone and tension are an essential part of health, inseparable from a free, easy expression of self. Where responses and spontaneity are stifled, so too is personal being and existence. The fears behind emotional tension usually relate to threatening figures or incidents from the past distorted and imported into the present so that the individual feels weak and helpless, gripped by an omnipotent but invisible giant.

All tension is a recreation and re-living of the past however recent the actual trauma or problem. Life itself may become a threatening situation with fear about loss of control and tension accumulating to overwhelming levels. Tension may be localised to a specific area, causing localised discomfort or it may be more generalised with symptoms in the whole body area.

Tension in the larynx may cause loss of voice, where a suppressed impulse to scream has affected one or both vocal chords, and all speech is diminished. The general quality of life may be reduced and modified by such localised problems in an attempt to control a response which may have been quite appropriate at the time. There is a natural wish inside everyone to give expression to the self. Where an unconscious drama from the past cannot be allowed an outlet at the time, then tension in the present may be the only alternative to a division of personality or more severe mental illness.

Every aspect of emotional tension is heightened and prolonged when combined with negative certainty or negative conviction. Such negatives create a self-destructive compromise and are profoundly limiting to individuality and growth.

Examples of Specific Negative Conviction which bring about Tension

1 I feel tense

2 I can't relax

3 I can't express myself properly

4 I cannot change and will always be the same

5 I am tense and it is getting worse with every contact

6 Other people see and sense my tension or malaise and dislike me for it

7 Others see me as weak because I am tense

8 Other people dislike me when tense

9 One day I shall die when I get so tense

10 There is an organic reason for my tension which the doctors have not found, or know and won't disclose

11 I am incurable.

On the Cure and Resolution of Emotional Tension

1 First clarify any distortions of yourself, especially the way you judge yourself in a new situation.

2 Start to rebuild confidence, beginning with a new situation, emphasing your ability to cope, survive, and to relate at the time.

Use your inherent natural ability and experience to overcome problems as they arise. Where the causes are of your own making, then the cure is also entirely within yourself. In some cases tension is caused or provoked by outside situations. Here, an outside support such as homoeopathy, relaxation, or yoga, may be needed to complete the cure.

3 Give more interest, and caring to others. Stop thinking so much about your own self-image and tension. Be more spontaneous, expressing yourself as you are and feel now. Think more of what you can give to others and less about their opinions. Accept tension as your limitation at present, but only a limitation, and not an unchanging disaster.

4 Stop seeing others as judges or a reflection of yourself. See them as people with needs where support and understanding is also

needed. Give as much as you can to help others. This inevitably strengthens and reinforces the positive within you at the same time.

5 Develop attitudes and interests which are more optimistic and positive. Base them on a clear awareness of your intrinsic creative abilities and gifts, to create more healthy attitudes and expressions.

6 Start to counteract your own specific negatives by positive specifics. List these as above and write down their detailed positive counterpart. Affirm the positive specific throughout the day so that it becomes a part of you and a habit. Accept the positive counter-thought as a true affirmation for you. Don't just see them as a gimmick because nothing will happen.

7 At all times try to understand the roots and unconscious motivations behind a symptom, especially the neurotic gains. Visualise yourself in a positive position to support its action to a maximum.

More General Notes on Tension-Solving

Aim to resolve any conflicts between drives, expectations, needs and fear. A frequent wrong assumption is that contact with others leads to criticism and fault-finding rather than stimulation of greater learning and more positive responses. At all times be sure that your attitude towards others is not harsh, judgemental, or critical. Be reasonably tolerant at all times, but not excessively so either.

Chapter eight

Concentration and Memory

Concentration

Concentration is giving undivided attention to a particular area of work, interest or study to create the optimum conditions for understanding, retention and memory.

On the Ability to Take-in Thoughts and Ideas

In order to concentrate with undivided attention, the individual must also be undivided psychologically. Concentration is undermined by emotion or the distracting stimulus of other unrelated thoughts or feelings. Interest and attention depend upon the psychological as well as the physical and both need to be in balance for optimum concentration.

On the Causes of Lack of Concentration

1 Ill-health or malaise – as during an acute illness such as flu, causing giddiness, nausea, impairs concentration, just as headache or pain in any part of the body. Problems like impaired hearing make concentration a strain and an effort – as much a problem for the child with chronic otitis after mumps as for the elderly with auditory nerve degeneration. In a similar way impaired vision from any cause puts additional strain on concentration. Other problems such as dyslexia limit understanding and add tension or strain because of the psychological overlay to the underlying reading problem.

Psychological causes are the commonest reasons for reduced concentration with anxiety, tension, lost of confidence and depression, commonly impairing attention. Most causes are due to limited confidence and fear. It can also occur in the confident bright child who is bored and irritable. Any disturbance in the pattern of the family or peer relationships blocks psychological input and expression, making for poor, weak image patterning and weak recall.

Depression, anxiety problems, obsessional control, lack of flexibility, fear, or excessive, competitiveness also undermine concentration and the retention of ideas. Over-emphasis in a particular area, perhaps excessive intellectualisation or emotional lability, similarly undermine memory and learning.

Pain distracts, and when severe, prevents adequate imprinting of a stimulus on the memory pathways. The causes vary from arthritis to dental neuralgia, migraine, gout, lumbago or renal colic. Medical diagnosis and treatment may be needed before concentration can be fully re-established.

Drugs which Undermine Concentration

These include the common addictive drugs, amphetamines, barbiturates, LSD, marijuanha, cocaine, heroin, solvents and glues. Drugs of pharmaceutical origin, including tranquillizers, sedatives, appetite suppressants, anti-allergics also reduce concentration because they dull mental functioning, alertness and receptivity. The social addictives, coffee, tea, nicotine and alcohol temporarily stimulate but there is usually a falling-off in attention and concentration, once the initial effect has worn off.

Environmental Factors that Undermine Concentration

These include high or low frequency noise and vibration, both having a profound physical and psychological affect upon intellectual activity. They unsettle and irritate, interfering with attention and stimulus imprinting. Any impairment of environmental harmony also undermines the abilility to take in and retain. For others, electro-magnetic waves cause malaise, with fatigue headache, poor concentration and memory disturbance and are as undermining as the more obvious noise and hum factors. Inadequate light also reduces concentration and thinking and a consistent exposure to artificial or inadequate lighting is a common cause of headache. Bad posture, poor positioning, a noisy, smoke-filled office, add further to concentration difficulties.

The spacing, size, position, colour, orientation and perspective of a room are all important for concentration. A damp basement with poor light and the impression of living below ground level can be as psychologically unsettling as a high-rise, top floor office. In general a well-proportioned room is an inspiration to learning and retention, a narrow, low room more of a barrier.

Stale air and tobacco smoke are physical and psychological irritants which undermine concentration in both the smoker and non-smoker. As far as colours are concerned, intense, brilliant reds disturb and provokes restlessness. The paler spectrums of green, pink and neutral cream, if not too intense, engender ease, relaxation and support optimum concentration.

Factors that Limit or Impair Concentration

When a whole society and culture is pressurised, politically and economically, then physical survival is a priority. A balanced diet with adequate calories, vitamins, trace elements and minerals is basic to health as well as thinking and concentration. Where media pressures or propaganda are intense, then judgement, differentiation, effective awareness and imprinting of imagery and memory signals can be significantly lessened. When feelings of provocation are strong and tend to stimulate resistance and fight, then concentration may become intensified.

Factors that Facilitate and Improve Concentration

Psychological and physical good health helps confident interest in the task or situation in hand. A balanced relationship with others, and the absence of severe stress at personal levels also facilitates maximum concentration.

Memory

Memory is the organisation of sensory, intellectual and imaginative patterns within the storage circuits of the cortex, so that there is availability for recall when needed. These circuits retain or release both immediate and associated past memory impressions when required. In health, memory has a broad spectrum of availability, flexibility and association. Illness, disease and sometimes medical treatment can provoke loss of memory, especially for recent events but the earlier past events are less vulnerable to loss or damage.

Definition

Memory is thought recall as and when it is required. It can be visual, photographic, or non-image forming. A variety of associated emotions and sensory impressions act as a trigger to it, but anything associated with the past can stimulate a review of a previous situation, or a revival of feelings associated.

Factors that Undermine Memory

1 Pressure of any type, especially of a stressful type.

2 Illness, physical or psychological, may undermine both vitality, and concentration with loss of interest, awareness and well-being.

3 Noise, distraction, any environmental factor which lessens attention, may irritate or undermine thought and concentration.

4 Boredom and lack of motivation.

5 Depression and indifference.

6 Fatigue, as from insomnia or after a sustained effort.

7 Irritability.

8 Alcohol.

9 Certain pharmaceutical drugs, especially those which sedate or tranquillize.

Factors that Facilitate and Improve Memory

1 Interest.

2 Motivation.

3 Psychological rewards – parental approval, the satisfaction of passing an examination, prospects of promotion, financial rewards.

4 Freedom from pressure and anxiety.

5 Psychological balance.

6 A supportive, happy, personal relationship.

The Recommended Approach to Improve Memory

In order to improve memory it is important to improve concentration. Other links or associations, strengthen recall, for example a colour, phrase or visual image. A poor memory can be improved by practice with careful attention to taking-in; more time for concentration, and active recall. Careful note-taking helps to fix the image and can be used as a key to recall. Try to understand what you are learning and why. Whenever possible clarify the origins, meaning, principles and philosophy when learning, in order to relate and integrate a part into a totality. Don't just learn parrot-fashion. Learn through understanding and association. For example, when learning a list of words or vocabulary, learn by association to other known, closely-related words or expressions – to hang the list together into a meaningful whole.

How to Improve Memory and Recall

Listen much more attentively and understand more of what is being said and studied. Make a few key notes at the time, and look through these afterwards to re-think what you have heard. Enlarge the notes where needed and retain them. Think as you listen, and try to develop other interests in the field to broaden and integrate what you are learning. When listening don't only be a passive recorder, but take in actively. Make positive associations to other areas and experiences. Understand and visualise what you are learning and are concentrating on. If you don't understand, stop and ask, or make a note to clarify it. Don't panic if you don't understand a part, or can't recall it later, but give more detailed attention to the whole. Develop links with other areas to broaden and familiarise. Try not to be dependent on back-ground sound for concentration, ultimately it is a distraction. After a lecture or period of study go over the material again to make sure you have understood the salient points and to facilitate recall. Broaden understanding by reading associated topics, to enlarge and deepen the links and associations. Discussion is another useful way of improving memory recall.

Further Useful Techniques and Exercises for Student Learning

Read a chapter or lecture and then note down as much as you can of the essentials. Note the key ideas, major sections, headings and conclusions. Actively recall your notes again after 4-6 hours and again the following morning or evening. Try not to confine yourself just to the limits of the lecture or subject. Aim to see more overall meaning and implications. Broadening interests fosters understanding and more of the flexible recall pathways. If necessary, use a cassette-recorder for notes, ideas and later recall. But don't rely solely on gadgets.

Examinations and Revising

Don't work up to the last minute before an examination. Give yourself a rest and relaxation period of at least 48 hours, to overcome fatigue and any stale feelings. If you still feel that it is vital to revise up to the very last minute and you can't relax, spend the last few hours revising in a general, overall way rather than looking and learning specific topics, hoping these will 'come up'. To support understanding and recall on the day, spend several weeks before any examination planning and going over the meaning of the syllabus. In this way, pressure in the last few days and weeks will be lessened. Don't over-learn in a parrot-fashion. Understanding is essential at each stage, whatever the subject matter, and more important than cramming facts in isolation. If you don't understand, ask, get clarification and help. Talk about the work and syllabus with others, your peers and teachers. Try to develop as much practical interest as possible. Never learn only a part of the syllabus. This is the best recipe for failure. Give special emphasis and learning to major, fundamental areas. There is a 'luck' element present in every examination, but don't rely upon it and usually 'spot' learning only intensifies anxiety and tension, lessening concentration recall.

Further Notes on Concentration and Memory

Look, listen, feel and understand at all times to sharpen concentration. Be original and creative in the way you think and learn, alert, dynamic, alive in your approach and associations for more imaginative, flexible learning. Don't be afraid to explore new techniques in memory retention, as long as they don't distract from the matter in hand or become too complicated.

The excessive pouring out of feelings and emotions, tends to undermine. Be more free with your mind when working, don't just try to pour facts into it. Memory development and learning should be part of an overall thought process and not separated from the rest of activity or from enjoyment. When distractions occur, accept and admit them, rather than opposing them, but resolve them as a problem to learning as quickly as possible. Try not to be ruffled or irritated. Memory without feeling is a 'dead,' uninteresting exercise, difficult to resuscitate. Lively interest and feeling at the time of learning gives memory a more lasting, dynamic quality because the mind is more alert as a whole and not only rooted in the intellectual. In this way the whole person is involved.

Chapter nine

The Importance of
Relaxation

Without exception, rest and relaxation are
essential to life and growth – as important at a
physiological level as a psychological one. A
pause is intrinsic to every physiological phase,
and after every contraction or effort, there is a
point of relaxation, however brief. Sleep is
man's most important replenishing period,
needed to rest brain and mind, but also
essential for the body as a whole.

Relaxation combats fatigue by facilitating
attitudes of letting go, and supporting the
excretion of toxic wastes as well as unhealthy
emotional attitudes. Man's physiological ma-
chinery is built around a phase of pause or ease
after effort, and this happens at every level,
from the primitive amoebic cell to the most
complex organism. During the phase of rest or
'dynamic inactivity', the cells are not inactive
but actively diffuse out waste material which
would otherwise accumulate and undermine

health. Elimination, revitalisation and replenishment occur during the rest phase. The cerebral cortex is most vulnerable to fatigue because it is most evolved, but less complex cells like those of muscle also need to be replenished when fatigued.

Relaxation is also the psychological state of letting go, a time to eliminate the psychological negatives which sap and undermine strength as much as any physical toxic matter. All tension holds in and opposes elimination, and natural growth.

Stress causes adrenalin release which adds to tension. Where relaxation is absent, tension and anticipation accumulate and form the inability to let go. An easy attitude supports health and release of strain. Relaxation helps the mind be less tense, and more available for creative work and leisure. When there is stress, relaxation is even more important, to limit its damaging effects.

The Role of Relaxation in the Build-up of Vital Reserve

Man remains healthy only because of regular periods of sleep, relaxation and quiet. Being deprived of rest quickly leads to illness, exhaustion and breakdown. For normal day to day functioning and health to continue, there must at some time be a prolonged rest pause during the 24-hour cycle, which varies with individual need, temperament and the physiological body clock. In general six hours sleep is a minimum requirement to allow reserves to build-up and for adequate elimination to occur. Anyone who is at all pressurised needs additional rest, a break during the day when he or she can just sit back quietly without interruption, with a ten or fifteen minutes 'flop' of mind and body, in order to cope and continue the day.

Letting Go of Problems

Life is a chain of challenges and problem-solving. It should not be exhausting however, unless drives and perspectives are wrong. As society in general becomes more pressurised and stress-laden due to rapid changes, the ability to let go, relax and forget, is even more important. Relaxation, prayer, or meditation, are different forms of letting go which allow a recharging of energies and more balanced perpectives. This is why for many people relaxation is also a form of healing.

Relaxation after Effort

Any major effort – psychological or physical exhausts to some degree, and rest is needed varying with each individual. The time needed after strain varies with age, health, constitution and general fitness. A brief pause may be needed or a more prolonged period of inactivity, according to the person and their level of fitness.

Relaxation and the Present Social Pressures

Living on the edge of a social revolution, and a time of social re-structuring, places some tension and stress on every individual. Where the involvements are direct, then rest and relaxation are even more important to maintain flexibility and health. Tension, anger, fear and uncertainty are best combated by periods of relaxation during the day to keep perspectives at realistic levels. Meditation techniques like T.M. (transcendental meditation) have shown that gains to health and creativity develop from deep states of relaxation.

Relaxation and Health

The consistent failure to make time for quiet, pause and reflection is major cause of ill-health and unrest in society today. Its importance cannot be over-emphasised. Letting go supports a more intuitive-creative approach to life and problem-solving, so that more formal, limiting aspects of the mind are less dominant.

Relaxation, the Under-valued Commodity

Relaxation is not a form of opting-out, nor being lazy. It is a specific, and essential dynamic pause for body and mind to let go of strain and to re-establish equilibrium. Claude Bernard defined this dynamic position as homeostasis or internal balance.

Exercises in Relaxation

1 Practise letting go after a busy period, finding a quiet spot and letting all tension and strain just drain out of you as you sit, spine straight in an upright posture. Practise this two or three times a day.

Whenever you can, be quiet and alone for a few minutes. Find *unpressurised* time for this exercise.

2 Flop out, lying supine, in the dead man's position. Let the body be totally relaxed and at ease. At the same time, the mind should be relaxing. Aim for a sense of weightless, floating relaxation.

3 Practise relaxing during times of activity, especially motorway driving or when under pressure.

a At the wheel, practise letting go of all pressure, unclenching the steering wheel. When tired, stop and rest. Nap briefly for ten or fifteen minutes before driving on. Never get into the habit of rush, dead-line driving when there is no need for it. Practise easing back at all times and whenever you can.

b Always take a reasonable lunch-break, away from the office environment. Eat a light adequate meal and don't talk shop or business during your break period. Whenever possible, get away, on your own, for a quiet stroll and take your mind off pressures, demands, and dead-lines.

Chapter ten

Achievement Potential (AP)

Achievement potential is the realisation of creative potential in a particular field of endeavour – physical, psychological, intellectual or artistic. We all need to express ourselves as we develop, to realise gifts, aims and potential – for personal satisfaction as well as a stimulus to further growth, new ideas and perceptions. When goals and directions become a tangible reality, ideas can be developed and plans put into action.

Developing Achievement Potential

AP can be developed by endeavour, hard work, determination and will-power, but other factors are also important. These include timing, visualisation, imagination and intuition which permit broader and wider steps to turn aims into reality. Vision and imagination support growth and change in a broad, flexible dynamic way. When less fixed or structured goals can be tolerated, this allows more imaginative movement and a less defined approach to outcome is possible.

Concentration and AP

The ability to be able to concentrate on an area of thought or stimulus and to maintain it long enough for meaningful associations and developmental ideas to occur is essential for the emergence of new ideas. Lack of sustained concentration, doubt or fear weaken initiative and exploration. Self-imposed limits and boundaries are applied, rather than less confining, imaginative or experimental ones. AP is the position of optimum growth at every level, and in this sense it is basic to every new change whenever it is occurring.

The Flexible Achiever and the Compulsive Controller

The flexible achiever can be tense, even impatient, at times and depressed but in overall attitudes he or she is relaxed, with a more total viewpoint. For AP to be realised, ideas and attitudes must be fluid and open.

Stimulus from any direction, in each situation, is something for consideration, possibly for rejection, but only *after* consideration rather than before. Compulsive controlling causes tense attitudes, fear of breaking rules and altering or changing existing patterns. There is too much insistence on a formal approach which creates a barrier to innovation. Change is accepted only as long as it fits into familiar patterns and known systems. The outcome is inevitably that AP and creativity are kept minimal because of under-lying resistance to new and different links and associations. New perceptions, the finding of alternative solutions is slowed down and in this way becomes more difficult.

AP and Sensitivity

The free flow of broadly associated ideas and feelings links AP to a more creative resolution of problems. Sensitivity and caring for others is psychologically inseparable from growth and self-realisation. New ideas initially often seem strange, even threatening. Greater tolerance towards innovation is inseparable from more open accepting attitudes towards self and others.

Where there is healthy growth, the need to control and prejudge each situation is not predominant. Happenings are accepted as they are, without insisting that they always conform to formulae, known assumptions and patterns. In this way a more overall healthy perspective develops.

Goals and Their Achievement

The optimum psychological conditions for goal and AP achievement are freedom from self-imposed pressures and narrow perspectives. Confidence without certainty, concentration as well as the ability to let go, supports more open non-prejudicial attitudes which make for health and creative goal achievement.

On the Time Needed for AP to Actualise as Goal-achievement

There are no absolute rules. Success depends upon each individual, goals envisaged and the steps or phases of change necessary to bring it into being. Time is required for body and mind to make the inner changes in energy, direction and vitality as well as in the outer situation for its expression and realisation. In treatment, I have found that a twenty-year condition can take up to one year to clear, provided that it is curable and treatable. When considering goal-defeating attitudes of twenty years duration or more, a year may also be needed to change and resolve blocks. The actual time needed may be much more or less, depending upon the aims, drives and priorities. Goals extend and develop as the individual changes – and this is healthy as long as the changes reflect new perspectives and ideas and not just change for the sake of changing or to avoid, or as an excuse for non-emergence. Where visualisation, interest, determination and drive are optimal, then the time needed for their realisation as concrete expressions is minimal. When drives are weak or changeable, lacking in concentration and direction, then any creative outcome takes much longer and is less certain.

Allowance for the Unexpected

For everyone without exception, life is an unfolding of the evolving new and the un-expected. Change occurs as part of every existence, and should be confidently expected. When the individual is relaxed, more centred, more him or herself, then the unexpected is not seen as a blow of fate or misfortune but as a bonus and an extension to the present. Where change is greeted with consternation and dismay then life itself becomes a negative, blocking growth and AP, because the mind is insufficiently receptive. Without exception, everyone needs to be more philosophic in their thinking when a change occurs, or something new takes place – in order to see it in true perspective.

You Are What You Think

Individuality, how you see yourself, relate to others, your perceptions, expectations, predictions and understanding are all the direct outcome of your psychological attitudes and the way you think. Where thought spontaneity is blocked by defensive interest, superficial attitudes or neurosis, then distortion, misperception and misunderstanding makes goal achievement more difficult. Where everything must conform to a known, already existing framework this dulls and diminishes everything including spontaneity of expression.

The Causes and Attitudes that Bring Failure

There is a saying that nothing succeds like success – because success engenders confidence, expansion of self, renewed effort and drive. Failure, accidents and mishaps often follow inner patterns of failure which perpetuate negative situations in an attempt to confirm their reality. Aims and goals are only negative when the inner reality has lost contact or denied the positive aims. Compromise directions and goals are often based on flight and weakness. Failure is only inevitable when it is the outcome of negative attitudes, negative certainty and negative visualisation.

Physical Causes of Failure and Low AP

Every undermined, neglected or weakened physical state needs treatment and correction to avoid dragging the imaginative, inspirational-creative drives down with it. Unless due to trauma or hereditary, a poor physical state is often the end-result of prolonged and destructive thinking or negative attitudes, which have de-vitalised and depleted reserves and weakened the physiological terrain. When correcting physical problems and deficiencies, it is also important to correct self-denigratory attitudes as well, so that the body can develop more harmoniously and positively to support creative achievement and realisation in general.

Psychological Causes of Failure and Low AP

Positive thinking, confident attitudes, definite formed ideas and imagery bring positive results and achievement because they are harmonious. Where goals and aims are negative, destructive, or self-orientated with no sensitivity to the needs or feelings of others, failure is inevitable because self-interest alone lacks the depth of energy and drive needed to bring them into reality. Persistence, confidence, concentration, optimism and faith make for successful goal-realisation. Anger, rage, resentment, and disappointment are inevitably a part of life's polarity and ambivalence. They are mainly negative and destructive when denied or suppressed. The acknowledgement at the time, of anger, rage or criticism supports spontaneity and is a part of freedom of expression. Some anger, and negatives are unavoidable and occur to some extent in every creative work or project. As negatives can never be totally eliminated, they should be given more open expression and be made more a part of the totality. In this way the dangers of suppression can be avoided. Without spontaneity of feeling – positive or negative, there can be no spontaneity of action. The major barrier to achievement is negative anticipation, prejudgement and repressed anger or rage.

The most Positive Mental Attitudes for Realising AP

Where there is an overall viewpoint, quiet, relaxed confidence, acceptance and awareness of the inspirational sources, realisation of potential follows, in its own unique and individual way. Much depends on the mental attitudes, less so the intrinsic gifts and abilitites, although both are important and to some degree both are present in everyone. For AP to work, you must also have clear-cut goals which you can visualise and believe in. In this way the energy behind the image is channelled into external shape and form, with each idea evolving into a part of the mosaic and a contribution to a new totality.

The Limitations of Self-hatred for AP

Negative, complaining attitudes, reinforce uncreative self-destructive attitudes and undermine creativity. Self-hatred opposes change and the new as it emerges and tries to destroy it. Attitudes of self-hatred and self-criticism also hide opposition to others because they symbolise change. The ego directs criticism and denial towards the self in an attempt to control and limit all movement. Attitudes of this type ultimately mislead and are defensive, leading to depression, illness and failure syndromes.

Fear, Guilt and AP

Unless guilt is appropriate and a positive part of reparation it is largely destructive. Rigid attitudes, imported from the past or from others feed a conscience which is more concerned with punishment and self-limitation than expansion and growth. Fear and guilt diminish because they attempt to base the present, on past phantasy asumptions and certainties rather than a dynamic evolving present. Guilt creates failure, futility and frustration by destroying confidence and drive. The emerging new, as a creative unfolding experience, becomes a target for guilt because it seeks to destroy the vulnerable present by masochistic attitudes and preoccupations. Without strong reparative drives, guilt nearly always becomes a barrier to the realisation and achievement of potential.

Why the realisation of AP is a Problem for Some

Failures occur because expectations are either unreal, inflexible or infantile in origin. There is failure to realise that achievement is the natural outcome of intention and drive, not some special talent or gift available to the privileged few. Basically AP is creative energy expressed through goal and achievement channels to form a coherent and tangible outcome. There is nothing magical or mysterious about new insights and visions. They are links and associations that develop naturally by accepting creative links, and not related to either speculative or contrived thought.

Accepting AP as a Reality

Creative force is the energy and movement inherent in each individual without exception. All change takes place from within, as internal drives and energies seek an external shape for their developing form. These external expressions vary in an infinite variety of ways, the creative drives stimulating the highest achievements of *homo sapiens.*

The humdrum, the mundane, the mediocre and failure are often the outcome of interference with the creative drives, affecting their free, spontaneous expression. Many run from growth and success because they fear its demands and responsibilities, staying in the wings of life, but also lacking the joys and satisfactions of a creative expression and life-style.

Routines, Habits and Fixed Ideas which are Destructive to AP

Routine thinking and conforming are attempts to halt the natural flow of life, the infinite kaleidoscope of underlying drives and urges. Routines puts boundaries upon understanding and thinking, much as attitudes of rigid certainty to insight. For this reason, try to limit fixed thinking and attitudes by more open sharing, discussion and dialogue.

Attitudes which Support AP

An overall approach to self and others allows maximum tolerance of new situations where familiar statements are less evident or even absent. With greater tolerance of new perspectives, new angles, new approaches, new thinking can also be allowed, leading to new ideas and goals.

When an achievement goal is clearly visualised, it will actualise, or develop tangible expression, because thought energy becomes matter or substance, when concentrated and sufficient time is allowed.

Opposition as the Expression of Different Attitudes and Perceptions

Where others differ, oppose plans or ideas, listen more and consider their viewpoint as a natural expression of difference and alternative. Because everyone comes from contrasting points of origin, difference and opposition are inevitable as well as desirable, helping correct narrow perspectives. Difference is often a question of sematics and language. Clearer, non-emotional words may be needed before there can be more sharing of aims, and ideas. Opposition should be valued, because it gives a chance to re-think a particular position although not necessarily changing it. Change and difference also stimulate some fear, opposition, hostility and resentment – because they are felt to threaten the familiar established order. Difference allows for an interchange of alternative, different views and positions, as long as there is not too much emotional pressure – which tends to negate the positive aspects. Few people like being disagreed with or can easily accept and listen to a different viewpoint. The difficulty of discussion between teenagers and adults is a good example of this. Both usually disagree and see the situation differently. The teenager is for change, dialogue and discussion, but over-intense attitudes often block any fruitful interchange.

Neurosis and AP

Neurosis is where fear undermines and dominates life and relationships. Energy evailability become limited, as neurosis seeks to impose its own rules, controls and reality, or to erect boundaries where there should be none. A softer, more balanced overall approach is diminished by infantile attitudes and a determination to stamp a particular viewpoint of the past on the present.

Creative Thinking for Problem-Solving and Inventiveness

Where drives are given expression without excessive emotion or pre-judgement, then more creative ideas, and imagery can form. There may be new insights and viewpoints in the scientific or artistic field with a break-through in problem-solving. These are the natural outcomes of AP provided that its expressions and outcomes are left to develop their own levels and form without judgement and interference. When they can be tolerated, the results are both unique and surprising.

Exercises in AP development

1   Clarify your goals in social and work areas and see clearly where and what you would like to be in one and five years time. Visualise the end result as already a reality, rather than the intermediate steps, and keep the image clearly in your mind as a *fait accompli*.

2   Visualise yourself clearly as having already attained your goal so that the mental imagery can exactly match the expected outcome.

3   Don't vary your goals once decided upon, and avoid constantly changing direction as this is wasteful, non-productive and destructive to confidence and creativity.

4   Refuse to allow negative doubts and uncertainty to enter into your mind. Never doubt success, once a goal is set, however illogical, or impossible it seems. You should have positive certainty and positive imagery in the forefront of your mind coupled with a relaxed confidence. Do not allow doubts and negatives to reinforce old failure patterns.

5   Practise daily being and feeling yourself at
    your target and goal. Act and believe the
    goal to be inevitable. Be certain that the
    end-results are ultimately positive, en-
    riching others and not imposing or limiting
    them. See yourself as giving, creating and
    supporting others with *their* opportunities
    and openings, as well as receiving from
    them.

6   See yourself as successful with others, to
    enable the end-result to be harmonious and
    in tune with your depths and deity.

7   Write your own exercise for AP de-
    velopment here.

Chapter eleven

Visualisation

Visualisation is the conscious linking of a visual image to a desired physical or psychological condition. It applies consistent thought energy in order to achieve change. The process creates the ideal conditions for growth, healing and movement provided sufficient time and concentration are given and there are no imposed limitations by doubt or fear. Intellect and logic are important to everyone and to the quality of our understanding – but they can also hamper development. Where the intention is growth or change of any type, sustained imagery of a desired effect can lead to dramatic changes as the image realises its object.

Dis-ease is the end result of negative thinking and destructive attitudes, the malaise further reinforced by negative imagery. What man has created, man can also cure and visualisation is undoubtely one of the most effective ways of achieving this, provided sufficient determination, time and energy are given to the process.

This ancient technique has had enormous success in curing physical disease, especially with cancer and its power has been demonstrated on many occasions over several decades in this field. Visualisation helps give clear cut aims and goals, supports healing energies and gives impetus to clearly defined programmes for change. Growth energies are inherent within each individual and are deeply rooted in the inspirational creative drives.

The General Value of Visualisation

Visualisation points psychological energies in a definite direction for development to occur in that particular sphere creating the optimum psychological conditions for change. Spontaneous cure and resolution can occur in any situation, no matter how apparently organic, 'fixed' and inevitable. Significant internal changes of an imaginative kind must always occur before the external changes take place. Visualisation facilitates physical or psychological change as long as the image is held with confidence. It provides the right psychological terrain for re-vitalisation especially where there has been damage or destruction. As the new visualised situation is accepted and becomes familiar, new energy patterns are released, and with them growth, repair and a new vitality.

Negative Visualisation

Many illnesses, both physical as well as psychological, are the direct result of long-term visualisation. The confident expectation and certainty of failure or illness brings this about. Negative attitudes always confirm their own object just as positive imagery confirm theirs. Energy, growth, development and momentum can be enhanced in a particular area to stimulate change, or it can be used to diminish and keep minimal according to the type of visualisation used. Distorted imagery makes for scattered growth, uncertain AP and weakened creativity drives. Concentrated, positive visualisation helps concentrate energy and makes for the best conditions for change.

Negative self-imagery is unfortunately very common in many attractive people who nevertheless hold negative views of themselves because they fear admitting the positive. This leads to stress and pressure which undermines looks and attraction and what is feared unfailingly occurs in one form or other. Development falters when there is wrongly directed creative energy, acting as a barrier to change. The threat of panic tension, anguish or spasm each time there is a possibility of change, also inhibits growth and goal achievement.

Suggestion

Suggestion is often confused with visualisation, but it is very different and generally far less effective in linking sustained imagery to goal achievement. It is less useful because suggestion give a less specific affirmation than the visual method and usually for a shorter period. Visualisation and suggestion techiques may be combined however to support and affirm positive specific aims. Where the underlying thoughts are of fear, the imagery attained is usually at the same negative level and the combination creates just this. The adage – 'nothing succeeds like success' is accurate because success, or the sense of achievement reinforces positive imagery and engenders further goal achievement. But failure begets failure too, as is well known in 'loser' attitudes. The mechanisms are exactly the same as for success, the creative stream does not concern itself with direction of drive, only its expression and form.

Exercises in Visualisation

1 Begin in a quiet room visualising a simple design or shape such as a square, triangle or circle. Visualise the shape first as white on a black background. You should be able to keep the image clearly in front of you for

several minutes. Later alter the colour arrangement and see it as black on white alternating the background colour. Practise for 5-10 minutes daily.

2   Change the image once you can hold it, to different shapes. See each clearly, see them small – the size of a small coin and then see them enormous, the height of a mountain.

Visualise the shapes chosen as coming into being, from a common centre. See each begin from nothing, becoming a particle, then a suggestion of form, finally developing a definite mature shape. Increasingly define it until it changes again and evolves into a new form of your own choice and complexity.

3   Visualise the above in colour too, once the black and white imagery has been mastered. Practise changing the colours from an initial spot of origin to the complete picture.

4   Visualise an object in your room such as a plant. See it as a seed or cutting at origin, in compost or rooting compound. Feel the temperature, smell the air, and sense the conditions required for growth. Then see the seed or cutting develop into a plant. Do the

same for something inanimate like an ornament. Visualise a painting then go back to the blank canvas, and see the artist creating it – first as an idea, then a sketch and finally the painting.

Visualise a chair, table or house in the same way, starting from the idea, of the artist, craftsman or architect and follow it through the sketch or drawing board, the plan, model and eventually the final object. See, feel and visualise each stage clearly.

5 Apply the same principles to a much larger object now, one outside the home, such as a ship, tank, bridge, train or car. Again see it on the drawing board and before that as the hint of an idea in the inventor's mind. If its origin was computer-designed, follow the graphics through each stage of design and manufacture to the present day. Follow it back after obsolescence and re-cycling to new origins – a new role and new purpose. An oceanliner or giant of the seas might fulfill a new role on retirement as a convention centre or land-based hotel.

6 Finally become the artist or designer yourself. Develop an idea however small or simple, into a sketch or plan, then into a concrete reality. Do this many times. Keep each attempt simple and straightforward. Complete each idea into a visual reality

before beginning another. Develop the visualised realities into concrete ones in those areas where you feel most inspired.

7 Write your own exercise for visualisition here.

Chapter twelve

On the Best General Approach to Problems of Emotional Tension

The basic concern of psychology is as much the relationship you form with yourself as well as to others. How you think, feel about yourself is inseparable from how you relate and get on with other people. In general when you are comfortable with yourself you are at ease with others. If you are uncomfortable, it is often because you have not fully accepted and come to terms with some aspect of yourself.

Discomfort may be the direct expression of a clash of personality and temperament, a confrontation, likes or dislikes or reflect tension anywhere within the spectrum of human emotion. In most cases however it is also because there are problems of self-image when only the concept of an ideal and perfect ego is acceptable. The reasons are not always conscious or clear but certainly ease and confidence are undermined by self-attack and self-criticism, which is frequently more important than criticism from others. The outcome is invariably dis-ease, tension and conflict. Some difference and divergence, either physical or intellectual is inevitable between two people who see, feel and experience differently. This is also positive and makes for learning, difference, interest, and individuality. The ability to accept divergence is a sign of health and because situations constantly change, so too do ideas, experience and their interpretation.

Principles of Self-help for Tension

1 Correct any tendency to displace feelings or drives, resentment, anger, hate, need, love or sexuality, into areas where their energy is bound or lost to you, and neither expressed nor realised. Such displacements are common in problems like agoraphobia, obsessional fears, anxiety and tension with the original emotional energy locked into a new threat or fear area. Psychosomatic problems are physical outlets for emotional drives which undermine health and may be a threat to health as in asthma or colitis. Try to keep problems and feelings much more available, on the surface and in the present where they have the best chance of being resolved without damage.

2   Keep self-imagery in balance and avoid negative, self-judgement and prejudice. When there are external problems like the fear of eating-out in company, shyness or phobias, find a rational understanding for their function, meaning, and psychological gains and why they occur.

3   When you accept yourself, you are likely to feel a lot more acceptable to others. This is clearly, although unconsciously communicated to them. Try to see the areas where you are not loving and accepting of yourself as you are. See where and how this can be corrected and changed.

4   Negative certainty and imagery is a major attempt to paralyse and maintain the psychological *status quo*. See this clearly and counter-balance them by the specific positive affirmation recommended. Never use a negative as you will further reinforce the problems.

5   If you are depressed – clarify its roots and origins. If there has been a past loss or unresolved guilt area, see how this relates, and is relevant to you today, the quality of your life and caring. The constant replay of obsessional-compulsive thought often hides

displaced rage, rejection or guilt feelings, with attempts to perpetuate an earlier, known and familiar situation, however painful at the same time.

Depression in adults often relates to depression in adolescence or childhood. Always clarify origins and any specific reasons for insecurity. Spend time analysing and understanding them – but never at the expense of involvement, enjoyment, or contact. Especially avoid becoming obsessional, excessively analytical, or intellectual about causes and reasons.

6 If you are still thinking, feeling and living a hurtful past, you are bound and fettered by old resentments and problems and not living and growing fully in the now. This is always limiting and self-destructive. It is vital to live in the present now for true health, growth and real satisfaction. Do not live on hopes and expectations, nor on past hurts, disappointments and losses.

Pain is part of life's inevitable learning experience. Live now, not within a yesterday or a future dominated by phantasy and expectation. Be positive. optimistic and caring in the now. The present is constantly changing and expanding and this is where you must be. Experience and give for health and happiness. The past forms the backcloth of your life and is your psychological heritage. Remember the winning moments, as well as the failures. When you recall hurts and pains see also their positive side and their stimulus to change, growth and maturity. Look forwards as well as backwards, not just in anger but with joy and gratitude as these are the ultimate healers.

Chapter thirteen

Coping with Divorce and Break-up

Every divorce is a painful experience in some way because it is a separation and an experience of loss. To avoid unnecessary suffering during the break-up, try to remain adult rather than excessively emotional or infantile. Feelings of intensity and provocation are common at this time but have little positive or practical value. Avoid attitudes of recrimination, blame and accusation because responsibility is always shared to some degree. Try to maintain self-confidence and to develop mature, friendly attitudes as much as possible. Remain centred and objective keeping resentment and tension minimal. Be friendly and courteous to your ex-partner and avoid falling into the trap of apportioning blame, as this is a further drain on confidence and vitality.

Accept the inevitable, when a relationship has ended. Realise that nothing lasts forever and that nobody owns another. Neither youth, health, children nor a partner belong permanently or by right to us, they are on loan or trust, so that we can give, value and care for them. See all life as an evolution, movement or transformation leading to new insight, growth, wisdom and development. Accept changes as they occur without too much comment or acrimony. In a modern pressurised society you cannot insist on certainties or take anything for granted, and this includes a relationship surviving permanently. Gratefully accept what you have received without infantile fretting or complaints. A separation outcome may be best for both of you and lead to new beginnings.

Every relationship is also like a child or a plant, and needs to be constantly fed and given to, in order to remain healthy. At the same time it must also be allowed to find its own form, shape, direction and outcome. When this can no longer happen, crisis and breakdown are inevitable, because every development and individuality must find its expression and cannot be contained within a rigid envelope of expectation or conformity.

You will need support and friendship to see you through the crisis however. Preferably confide in someone who will support and understand, without emotional demands or emotional involvement. A precipitate relationship at this time usually leads to further pain and hurt. During the actual divorce crisis you are unlikely to handle a new relationship well because of the infantile resurgence which deepens needs and demands. Many women have a close woman friend to help them over the crisis, but men are less good at forming such relationships and a colleague relationship is rarely ideal for sharing the anguish of pain and distress which occurs. If the divorce is the outcome of an amicable agreement without emnity or bitter feelings, then there are not usually severe emotional problems. But this is not very common, and most couples don't handle the ending or breakdown of a relationship in an adult way. An emotional crisis in one or other of the partners is exceedingly common, as infantile, immature demands and complaints come to the surface.

Where there has been no real love or caring for years, the parting may be a relief, a matter of financial agreement only. But for most couples the break-up is the end of something important and is painful. Even where one partner is committed to another, waiting to re-marry, and divorce a technical practicality only, there are nevertheless feelings of vulnerability, and sadness. Some guilt and attachment may remain for many years. In general there are few divorces that are not felt as a deep personal loss and a trauma with feelings of guilt or failure.

The key to coping with divorce is to stay in balance as much as possible by:-

1 Physical or artistic expressions to help counteract excessive analysing, intellectualising or emotional over-reaction.

2 Close friendships, to help give a better balance and perspective, for support as well as company.

3 Periods of stillness, especially quiet meditation without post-mortem obsessional thinking are of great value during the separation crisis.

4 Physical relaxation supports mental relaxation and should be encouraged.

5 Quiet, music, rest and relaxation with a closeness to nature supports psychological balance and overall perspective so that the divorce and separation can be seen more as an opportunity for a fresh start, for new developments and new beginnings.

Chapter fourteen

Mood Swings

Mood swings are movements in mood, with or without external provocation from a plateau state into a high or low intensity emotional state.

Where a hysterical temperament is also associated, the swings may be wild, with highs of elation alternating with troughs of despair. Never at ease in a social situation, or finding peace of mind, free to be themselves, there is a compulsive need to over-play and dramatise every situation. Beneath the mood swing is the fear of falling flat or becoming a bore.

All mood variation is normal and 'pancake' sameness is as much a symptom of disturbance as excessive fluctuation. The degree of variability depends upon a variety of factors, both physical and psychological, including the menstrual cycle, seasons, time of day, pressures, fatigue, blood sugar, lead and carbon dioxide levels as well as any emotional factors present. Where there is organic disease, or endocrine disturbance as in thyroid disease, the over-activity may cause restlessness, moody impatience, and short-fuse reactions. An under-active gland results in a sluggish, flattened mood, delayed responses, and the absence of spontaneity in general.

Hormonal changes, acting through linking channels in the mid-brain are a common cause of mood swings in pre-menstrual tension when impatience, irritability and intolerance contrast with strong needs for closeness, affection and dependency. Such swings are also common at the menopause, in men as well as women. Flights of mood, rage or tears may follow in rapid succession because of the psychological instability engendered by the hormonal changes. Chronic indigestion and peptic ulcer are more the end result of suppressed mood swings rather than a cause, with true feelings bottled-up under controls and superficial equanimity, stimulating acidity, spasm and damaging to the healthy mucous membrane. Where the basic temperament is unstable, any unknown situation can provoke a mood swing, sometimes quite violent and only afterwards is there a backlash of depression, guilt, exhaustion or collapse.

Any infection with a swinging high or intermittent temperature can also cause mood changes, especially in young children from a throat or ear infection, the pain or delirium causing restlessness and irritable outbursts. A similar, violent mood-reaction may also follow a sudden psychological trauma, where there has been shock, damage, or loss of functioning in any way.

Iatrogenic, or doctor-induced mood swings are becoming increasingly common, as allergic responses to many of the modern synthetic drugs. A 'high' is quite common after steroids or prolonged treatment with certain vitamins and a 'low' is common with children on antibiotics or anti-allergic decongestion treatments. Where there is allergy or sensitivity to colorants and dyes, in the tablet or capsule coating, these can also provoke mood disturbances.

Other related factors which affect temperament, and provoke mood changes leading to irritability, are insomnia, tears or depression, the exposure to prolonged irritating noise in the office or home, or inadequate natural daylight. Fatigue, low blood sugar (hypoglycaemia) and alcohol are other causes. Chronic allergic states – hay-fever, migraine and sinusitis may also provoke mood change. High atmospheric levels of pollen, dust, or smoke and central heating aggravate psychological conditions as well as causing a physical imbalance.

Psychological Changes which Cause Disturbance

Sustained psychological pressure of any kind inevitably causes mood variation. Tension, fear, uncertainty, lack of information in a work area, can also provoke anxiety, tension, loss of control, mood swings, depression and irritability. A physical assault often upsets mood stability for some time, leading to 'startle' reactions, loss of confidence and nightmares. Constant changes of environment are inevitable for pilots and airline hostesses and are another factor in mood change from the continual contrasts of time-zone and climate. These affect both mood and hormonal functioning. In men this may manifest as raised blood pressure, peptic ulcer, or irritable tension states. In women amenorrhoea (absent periods) is common as well as mood disturbances.

The underlying psychological mechanism is an overpressurised psychological situation, one which suddenly bursts out into an upturn of mood, followed by a 'downer' to escape from intolerable pressures. Such mood blow-outs rarely support mature problem-solving so that all too often the condition recurs again.

Mood swings are expressed physically as well as emotionally by spasm, colic, indigestion and insomnia. The swing attempts to reach a 'safe' psychological position of invulnerability and dissociation. A depressed flat state is the usual companion to an ecstatic high but the 'downer' which follows, is far more lasting than any state of elation.

Pain, either the threat or memory of it, as occurs in an anniversary reaction may also inflate one aspect of the psychological ego in an attempt to find an easy exit by a swing up into unreality and elation. But there are no lasting 'highs' and the split or alienation from reality causes its own problems, the outcome often one of increased uncertainty and lack of confidence.

Reality appraisal, judgement and problem-solving in the present are all lessened by mood-swings with reality decisions made more difficult because of lethargy, indifference or remoteness.

The psychological ego, which in health conducts appraisal, sensitivity, judgement, understanding and perception, loses most of its functioning when a mood swings occurs. Confidence, a sense of existing and being in the present is lost as reality and judgement are reduced. Physical weakness is a common side-effect of mood-swings and may cause anxiety about loss of control, fainting or fear of collapse.

In terms of confidence and experience, the price paid for recurrent mood swings is heavy. The gains are fleeting – mainly elation, denial, and obliteration, but these too quickly falling back again into depression and despair. A down-swing can be a hard one to reverse and sometimes seems irreversible. The major problem of the depressive swing is flight into another high which creates the chronicity, rather than bringing relief and a solution to the mood problem.

Exercises to Help Reduce Mood Swings

1 Initially, practise periods of relaxation for 15-20 minutes a day on three separate occasions. Flop in a quiet area. Imagine yourself either floating or sitting in a favourite relaxed spot. Continue this for several weeks until it becomes natural and deep.

2 Next practise being quiet and relaxed when elated, but take no important decisions or major financial commitments at this time. Whenever you are keyed-up, tense or excited, practise quiet sitting and meditating until the mood passes.

3 In a low mood-swing, practise more open attitudes, more giving and more contact with others. Practise talking and be more attentive to others. Don't only talk about yourself or your problems, but listen to others. Be more spontaneous, giving, and really caring. Also be physically active as part of a regular, daily work-out. Walking

or swimming is excellent, as long as it is part of a regular exercise programme and not excessive or part of a 'high' phase.

4 See clearly the factors which trigger-off mood swing. If there are problems, which you have not admitted or dealt with, then deal with them now. If you spot a 'trigger' area and repetitive stimulus to mood change, then look at it more closely and make changes in basic attitudes. This is important whenever earlier attitudes have been overtaken by changes and events, but where you have stayed static as in the original situation.

5 Use dreams as focal points of entry into deeper, more imaginative thinking. Write them down. If they have a relevance to mood-swings develop insight and under-standing along the path they suggest. If your dreams don't give clues to under-standing, still use them to phantasise and expand imaginatively. Record your dreams whenever they are remembered and use them as a springboard to new insight and change.

6 Be more imaginative in general, both in your mind and on paper. Develop new ideas by painting, drawing, modelling, working with clay, or plasticine. A non-verbal

creative phantasy-expression should be practised daily. Be daring in these self-expressions, and always experiment with new ideas, art and expressive formats. Be bold and express feelings, needs and emotions in this way, to reduce the need for psychological flights and emotional swings.

7 Write your own exercise here to help reduce mood-swings.

Chapter fifteen

Depression and the Blues

Within every psychological situation there are a variety of responses and feelings possible. These occur as the situation unfolds, each having a meaning in terms of anticipation, past experience and the actual present. In general, the intensity of a feeling-reaction, particularly a depressive one depends upon the overall state of psychological health, and how much the present is felt to contain and express concern and caring.

Depression other than that of grief, stems from an overwhelming reaction of self-hatred that excludes love and caring. There is an absence of secure contact with the deeper self. and its potential for healing and balance. This causes loss of faith and a sense of alienation so that at times life seems to have little point. Everything seems an effort and a chore without hope or the possibility of change because of the self-destructive attitudes, but also because of alienation from identity, the true self and from love and caring. Depression has too often been categorised and labelled but with little real meaning to the patient unless the causes are explained and understood. Some of these catagories are discussed in the following sections.

Reactive Depression

Reactive depression is usually described as caused by an obvious shock or trauma, which has triggered-off a depressive mood swing. Trauma does not however always lead to depression and sometimes an aggressive response is more common. An acute depressive reaction has often been preceded by a string of similar episodes, in a minor key over the years which prepared the soil for a more violent reaction and acute depressive state. The true cause nearly always lies in the past. Healthy attitudes help resolve present-day pressures in a more flexible way with humour and optimism. A divided past makes all of life's vicissitudes seem a weight and a depressing demand.

Endogenous Depression

This is another standard grouping of depression. The causes are thought to lie within the physiological structures, where imbalance is directly linked to psychological mood changes.

For many, whether there is a reactive or an endogenous depression, the external manifestations are those of an internal problem rooted in isolation and loneliness with electrolyte or other physiological changes very much secondary to the deeper causes. A feeling of being bereft, or of personal anguish, even non-existence is characteristic of the depressive mood. Isolation can also be deeply painful and occur within a family situation, even when surrounded by others, leading to added hopelessness and despair.

Social Depression

This is another label linking social, and environmental problems to depressive mood or illness. The inability to find work, redundancy or closure can cause anxiety and tension as well as depression because there is failure to appreciate the advantages and positives inherent in every change as well as the negatives. Where there are more open attitudes to difference, evolution and change, then creative problem-solving can occur. New ideas, more imaginative solutions and developments cure depression and are also a stimulant to health.

Existential Depression

Existential isolation is sometimes described as a cause of depression. To some degree, everyone is on their own, in a state of loneliness, isolation and anguish – however close the family ties. Awareness of our intrinsic isolation and vulnerability, the common failure to *fully* contact and communicate, may become associated with depression. Such depression is misplaced because there is failure to realise that we are always alone to some degree, however close to another. We also separate because some experiences, especially the deeper ones have to be felt and experienced alone.

A crisis of existence occurs when there is insufficient appreciation of our intrinsic links to a divine-inspirational, greater self and the enormous potential for original expression and health which this gives.

Post-Infective Depression

This is another common label applied to depression following an acute illness such as influenza. There is always some lowering of both vitality and mood. Glandular fever, hepatitis, hay-fever, sinusitis and tuberculosis are other conditions which provoke a 'low' in mood reaction. Where there is additional weakness and exhaustion, there may be insufficient strength of will to recover. In some cases pain, fever, or a toxic state, depletes vital efficiency and synthetic, non-biological drugs, further weaken resistance. A gap is created between the physical and the psychological which is expressed as depression. Thinking and functioning become increasingly superficial, or infantile so that eventually only a thin shell of the self is left functioning. In every infective condition, staying close to psychological perspectives and depths, helps prevent alienation and depression during the treatment period and encourages a swifter return to health.

The 'Mid-Life Crisis'

This is a term applied to men and women who develop depressive symptoms in the age range of thirty-five to fifty. A variable degree of depression is present at every developmental stage, from infancy onwards but it often comes to a peak at forty, when major hormonal and physical changes begin into occur. Together with a sudden awareness of age, there is a feeling of increased vulnerability, deterioration and change. There may be a sense of time wasted and lost, of mistakes made, or futility and failure with minimal acknowledgement of maturity, success, development, achievement and experience.

Marital crisis or relationship breakdown is common in a desperate quest for endless youth, sexuality and reassurance as the realities of infantile and adolescent omnipotence finally come to roost. At the same time there is a preoccupation with appearance, youth, and externals rather than deeper, more overall perspectives. The superficial concerns lead to disappointment and a sense of failure, becoming a source of dissatisfaction and then depression.

Puerperal Depression

Here, a more severe depressive illness develops after a confinement. During pregnancy all hope and life has been invested in the growing infant germ so that the essence of creativity is felt to be divided off as the child separates. At birth the life-force is felt to be lost with the child leaving the mother bereft, disappointed and empty – her creative ability gone with the child at the end of the pregnancy. She may feel like an empty shell, without feeling, yet guilty because she is depressed and other mothers are full of joy. The baby may also be resented or rejected, seen as the reason for her illness and because maternal feelings are initially ambivalent, guilt builds up. Resentment, jealousy fear and guilt add profoundly to any depression because part of the self is felt to be rejected within the infant and a cause of sadness. The process of motherhood may be carried on perfectly adequately, albeit mechanically, but lacking in joy, so that fatigue and tension-insomnia build-up adding exhaustion to depression.

Depression sometimes comes from negative thinking, distorted expectations, and a shock or illness during pregnancy. Problems occur because pregnancy is always a time of profound psychological change and adjustment. Depression with clear-cut reasons is usually mild in nature and only rarely causes severe problems. In a few cases, a severe trauma may cause illness, sometimes of a very disturbed mental nature, but where underlying attitudes are healthy, then the mother usually remains healthy too.

Usually the maternal experience of closeness, feeding, and caring for the baby acts as a stimulus to health and balance. When breast-feeding has not been possible, this is a loss to the mother, although not usually a conscious one. Bottle-feeding gives adequate psychological closeness to prevent problems developing in the child, provided it is given with warmth and tenderness.

Separation at an early stage is undesirable, unless absolutely necessary for surgical or medical reasons. When the process of postnatal psychological uniting does not occur naturally between mother and infant, there may be an underlying psychological problem preventing it. An unreal, psychotic state can be an attempt to find a solution to a painful reality. Distortion of self and identity causes changes in perception and judgement, and when this happens confusion occurs and with it fear, depression and breakdown.

Exercises in Overcoming Depression

1 Since depression is always self-generated, first clarify any negative attitudes which set-off a depressive mood. Once you are clearer about your own role, you will probably find that this is a longstanding pattern, a familiar way to avoid the threat of new situations or relationships, and having to change existing viewpoints and attitudes.

2 Where negative certainty is involved in a depressive problem with depressive imagery, use specific opposite affirmations to lessen and neutralise rigid assumption or conviction. Make the affirmations quite specific for you and the depressive negative which you are repeating to undermine yourself.

284

3 Practise letting-go of negative thoughts and self-destructive ideas. When these occur, get out of yourself, your habitual psychological stance by a change of environment for a few hours. Do something different. Look, listen and contact others. Especially listen to others, and not always to your own negative thought-patterns.

4 See the origins of depression through these patterns, when, and how they began. They are often remote although the feelings associated are strong and intense. Feelings re-activate old scars and resentments so that they can never be quite forgotten or forgiven. Impulses of anger, hatred and revenge cause depression far more than the actual hurts and traumas of the past. Practise giving up and letting go of old resentments. Visualise a healed, better relationship with the personalities concerned, and make this a reality.

7 Keep regular quiet contact throughout the year with nature. Whenever possible, walk in a park, garden or the country, listen, look and enjoy. Quiet listening has powerful healing, therapeutic and balancing qualities.

8 Write your own exercise for depression here. Keep it simple.

Chapter sixteen

Anniversary Reactions

Anniversary reactions are strong evidence for the underlying influence of the unconscious on the physical and psychological processes, as well as emotional balance and health.

Such calendar reactions are unconscious reactions to past events. They may be physical or emotional, and like the dream, they are a compromise, seeking to both express and prevent the break-through of too much feeling – in case it rekindles pain, feelings or memories.

When such reactions occur, there is a 'low' of mood and energy, sometimes a physical problem of indigestion, insomnia, fatigue, 'lumbago' or accident-proneness. They nearly always occur at a time of day, month or year associated with the original situation, and act as a trigger to the release of repressed emotion.The original event may have occurred many years before, or be more recent. At the time, reactions, feelings of rage, grief or tears were not fully admitted, so that they constantly recur, until there is an outlet or some resolution of their psychological energy.

The unconscious logic is both ageless and timeless. Yesterday and today are the same on the psychological clock or calendar. Memories and associations of the past are felt to be happening in the present and the immediate, because unconsciously there are no time boundaries and both past and present are intermingled. June 1940 could equally be June 1980 in the unconscious and felt just as clearly.

A shock or loss may be re-experienced vividly each year, although the conscious links with its origins are not always seen. Depression, irritability, and exhaustion are common symptoms, but pain or spasm may also occur. There may have been reactions of this type over several years, only ceasing when a link is made between consciousness, memory and feelings and the underlying, bound emotion is released.

An anniversary reaction differs from simple recall of a past event because of the strength of feelings associated and that the actual memory is usually unconscious, or expressed in indirect ways. The individual concerned has no idea what is happening or 'wrong', although friends and family usually know the true events and causes. Once a link with the past and the feelings associated is made, there is usually a full cure once the trapped emotional energy is released.

Guidelines to the Self-treatment for Anniversary Reactions

1 If you have a recurrent physical or emotional problem which flares-up year after year at the same time, consider a possible unconscious 'anniversary' reaction as a cause.

2 Try to think back each year through the key events of this particular time, especially those, associated with hurt, loss or pain. You may suddenly recall, or catch a glimpse of them in a dream or daytime association. These sudden, 'forgotten' glimpses are usually of particular importance and significance.

3 Ask close friends and family to help when symptoms occur, and listen to the links with the past they suggest. Take their suggestions seriously and think them through because you may be trying to block-out any memory and feelings involved, rather than come to terms with them.

4   If something important happened in the past, which was traumatic but is now without feeling, don't try to force it up into the open. Think it through quietly and allow for spontaneous expression in your own time. You will need to allow feelings and associations to emerge, but you should not pressurise them, or be in a hurry. In general, I do not recommend hypnosis for anniversary recall. It is better to allow the unconscious blocks to come up by themselves spontaneously, rather than trying to make them come up as this can create other or new problems.

Chapter seventeen

Anorexia Nervosa

This is the end result of a chronic condition, more common in young women than men. Typical symptoms are periods of alternating, compulsive eating followed by crash dieting, to the extent of regurgitating food or provoking vomiting in an attempt to reduce weight. There is a constant pre-occupation with body image, especially the fear of becoming obese, with an obsessional idealisation of being slim and underweight. Body-weight may fall to danger levels for normal physiological functioning and the constant swings between compulsive eating and dieting can cause weight swings of 3-4 stones in the same year. Body weight can fall as low as six stones or less. A delusional element is common in anorexia and sometimes a schizophrenic illness is also associated.

Obesity may be a family disease and not uncommonly the fat image of parents or relatives serves as a model for the disturbed body imagery. Sometimes the parents or grand-parents have themselves been over-preoccupied with food, weight, and diet, setting an unhealthy pattern for future generations.

Body image is distorted because of past patterns of eating, so that the individual sees him or herself as fat and large even when underweight. The image of a fat self dominates all rational thinking and motivation, undermining relationships and psychological growth. The menstrual periods are usually absent or weak. Sometimes there is amenorrhoea for months after a return to normal bodyweight. The anorexic personality is also unpredictable, emotionally immature, deprived of enriching contacts and interest which stimulate growth and health.

Because of displacement and distortion of self-imagery, the whole psychological self-portrait becomes unacceptable and uncomfortable, with depression intensified by an inadequate diet as well as unhealthy attitudes.

Rarely comfortable, when eating, and full after a few mouthfuls, the anorexic experiences distaste and revulsion for food. The powerful association of food and eating with a gross, inflated self-image, creates an obsessional component which perpetuates the problem.

The constant projection of energy and drive into food and weight-preoccupation, sensitizes the mouth and intestinal areas, creating fears of being trapped. Unable to give out, they feel stifled by feelings which they cannot express. A sense of failure occurs because all relationships tend to be partial and weakened by the physical and psychological immaturity.

Case Report

A girl of 20 came five years after a severe anorexic problem. Her body weight was now normal and she felt in full control of the problem. At times, she still had bouts of compulsive eating, but these were becoming less and she no longer had any compulsion towards anorexia or dieting. Her problem was her periods which had not returned and that body fat had failed to reform in some areas.

There was a loss of orbital fat in one eye socket, giving it a sunken impression, and both thigh areas were flattened. She had not fully recovered her normal body fat, but otherwise felt well and fit. The case illustrates a good psychological resolution of an anorexic problem, but shows how residual physical problems can still be present five years after the anorexia has ceased.

Self-help for Anorexia

1 Behind every anorexic problem there is a deep-seated confidence and self-imagery problem. Try to see yourself more honestly and clearly. Clarify your underlying insecure areas, even if you can't enlarge or develop them at once. Discuss problems of self-doubt feelings with others, especially a close friend or relative. Try to see just where you have blind areas and why.

2 Anorexia is usually associated with immaturity. If this makes sense, then see where you are still being infantile and clinging to childish wants and needs. Work out a plan to resolve and improve them. Discuss this too and tell others of your plans, and what you intend to check or change.

3 See why and how you binge, and what starts it off. Understand the precipitating causes, and how you react to frustration. Try to deal with them differently and more positively in the future.

4 Get information from your local library on the dangers of anorexia and low body weight. Join an anorexic group. Be better

informed about how you are endangering and undermining your health by anorexia.

5 Look carefully at your libidinal and sexual development. If there are denied problems in this area, discuss them openly. Mix as much as possible, making contact and friendships with both sexes. Clarify any overt problems of competition or rivalry with others especially those involving the close family. Try to discuss this more with the actual persons concerned in an adult way.

6 Write down your own exercise for anorexia here.

Chapter eighteen

Nervous Breakdown

Definition

Breakdown is the inability to cope and contain the feelings associated with a particular emotional situation or set of circumstances. A problem may be centred at home or in work, but where it is felt as a constant pressure of over-whelming feelings, this can lead to an inability to contain them. The absence of an emotional response, with depression, withdrawal or apathy can also occur and be just as disturbing as an excessive reaction, because nothing feels real or can be responded to.

Meaning

In a nervous breakdown, uncontrollable feelings emerge, both direct and often excessive because their defensive covering is overwhelmed by their intensity. The refusal to pretend and deny any further is often the first stage of breakdown, the patient at the 'end of their tether', no longer able to to deceive themselves or others about the real extent of their feelings. This letting-go is a positive event, although not always immediately obvious, and gives hope of coming to terms with the underlying emotional problem. The change is feared to be one for the worst, but this is not the usual outcome and on the whole a shift in emotional dynamics heralds a positive outcome.

Breakdown often means 'break-out', rather than the opposite, as pent-up feelings, forced down, suppressed and denied for too long emerge into consciousness. The reasons for such denial are many, including upbringing, family, social pressures and temperament. 'Break-out' is frightening when the underlying situation is charged with emotion of an infantile kind, leading to fear of violence, loss of control, guilt or punishment. This happens especially when feelings have been suppressed over a lifetime into a conforming temperament, lacking in complaint and self-expression. Tension and anxiety may be felt as something tangible within the body, wanting to burst out, yet at the same time outside the self and not familiar.

The feeling of being different, out of control causes additional problems and can be an added cause of anxiety because 'control' has always been the norm. The essential shift from a state of previous control to one of letting-go is one of the most positive factors in breakdown as well as most frightening because emotion and feelings come out with so much energy. With greater individuality and more authentic behaviour, there is greater potential for growth and change.

Once the causes and mechanism of 'break-out' are understood, there is enormous relief and a letting-go of tension. The realisation that every breakdown is a breakdown of weak unhealthy defences, into greater saneness, not a break-out of chaos, is important to understand. Once accepted, strong feelings like anger and resentment can be discussed or expressed with less drama. They lessen and diminish because it is the degree of suppression which aggravates and perpetuates them, rather than the feelings themselves.

Typical Symptoms

These vary enormously with each individual, his or her temperament, culture and background. In general there is a sense of being oppressed by feelings or events and not able to contain and cope with them fully. Compromise or change in a particular situation or relationship seems impossible.

Depression is common with tears, sadness or grief but equally there may be overwhelming tiredness, fatigue, lack of energy, appetite and drive. An 'all gone' empty, weak feeling occurs and bed-rest may seem the only way to survive for a time. Madness, death or collapse often feel imminent adding to fear and sometimes like a retaliation for letting-go.

Tension provokes palpitations, a rapid heartbeat, sweating, sometimes collapse or fainting in any part of the body, with cramp or spasm. There is a low tolerance of irritation, especially for noise and vibration. The urgent priority is to relax and to re-think the crisis, so that a shift in feeling can resolve a seeming impasse, which is the commonest cause of the crisis situation.

Every situation must be bridged and dealt with, however trivial at the time. If left they accumulate and cause anxiety. It is new, and different areas which are most difficult to cope with. But once a start has been made to tackle them, they become more 'ordinary' and easier to resolve. Where the real feelings are left un-expressed, and there have been no real fundamental changes, the problem may alter from an acute to a chronic one.

A return to health and normality only occurs when there is an open admission of the emotional feelings associated, leading to change and a strengthening of personality. Maturing only occurs when feelings occur in a more integrated way giving gains to internal security. These are essential changes that pre-vent a similar breakdown occurring at a later stage.

Temperament and Breakdown

A rigid, over-perfectionistic attitude towards the self, usually means that others too must be perfect and ideal. There is difficulty in accepting others as real people and inevitably there are many casualties in relationships. With such rigid models of self and others, unreal perspectives and viewpoints develop, because of the need to make reality conform to a static model. This is a common cause of many frustrations, problems, and difficulties.

A more relaxed temperament allows for more variation, difference, and more choice at every level. Problems are areas which need greater clarification and discussion, not necessarily agreement but essentially the spontaneous expression of feelings and opinions as they occur. Where attitudes are closed, based on collusion and denial, greater listening and understanding are needed to limit unreal expectations and fears. Feelings of pain, hurt and rejection are always a natural part of everyone's experience, but they should not be allowed to overwhelm or dominate the totality. In this way fear can be more accepted as a part of the whole spectrum of life. Rigid thinking and intense certainty are often associated with an obsessional temperament and can only be lessened by looking much more at the realities as they occur rather than as they might be. The boundaries of every problem, which involves feelings, must be confined to the now, in that way they can be dealt with in the present and resolved through a reality approach. Any other way only leads to uncertainty, anxiety and fear because only the existing present can challenge phantasy imagery and put it to flight by being reality-based and centred in the now.

How to Cope with Nervous Breakdown

1 Don't attempt to hide or deny your feelings or difficulties, however strong, frightening or out-of-keeping they may seem. Get help, and start to talk about them. Help need not necessarily come only from the professionals. Often the best person is a friend

or a relative, and always *try* to discuss it within the immediate family, unless this is the major conflict area and there is no opportunity for dialogue and sharing. You may feel however that you don't want to burden your partner or family with such problems. But find someone you like, can trust and feel close to – even if you have not seen him or her for years. In general, feelings, however strong and any related tension are always best out in the open. Once there is someone to talk with, be quite open with them and decide together what to do next, and if you need professional advice and support or not. When necessary, usually a counsellor, doctor, community worker or priest is most helpful but talking it through with a trusted friend may be sufficient and enough to re-orientate you again. If in doubt wait and see. Any increase in tension, anguish, insomnia or fear after talking and exploring may mean you need more time, rather than specialist help. Make time for feelings to emerge and the roots and causes of a pressure situation to be clarified. You may not understand just what has brought you to 'bursting' point because you are blocking and probably intolerant as well.

2 Try honestly to admit the true causes of your feelings and how unbearable tension originated, and the *reasons* why. It is likely that initially you will see no clear solutions, no logic for what caused the breakdown and

more thinking is needed because of your own blocks to perception.

If there has been a previous breakdown or crisis, the present situation is likely to be related to it in some way. The previous breakdown may give the link or clue to what is really happening beneath the surface, the roots of the problem and any connections with earlier events or traumas, possible from childhood. In general a sensitive friend who has known you well over the years is best able to point-out major blindspots and to give pointers where the problem has arisen. Causes are not just past hurts but also because of subsequent resentment, rage and denial. Such reasons are often clear and obvious once admitted, not always so unconscious or deep-seated that complicated unravelling techniques are required. Where large areas of feeling and emotion have been isolated or repressed over months or longer, they lack sufficient energy to fully discharge themselves and to find relief and outlet. Denial of a problem may be because of lifelong attitudes of self-denial and repression rather than a recent shock or trauma.

Excessive self-protection, anxiety and the fear of precipitating a crisis are other causes. Try to avoid denial as much as possible in your attempts to diagnose the reasons why, and always resolve difficulties now rather than in the future. When there is a breakdown situation, tomorrow is too late. Keep yourself and your psychological options as open as possible at all times for new learning, new perspectives and opportunities to occur.

3   Understand the meaning of breakdown and why it has occurred now – at this particular time. Don't think too much about the meaning of specific symptoms, they are usually the end-results and surface-expressions of the deeper inner feelings. Because the real self is blocked in expression and growth, such symptoms are usually only compromise expressions, a cause of pain but rarely major factors in their resolution. Building trust, dialogue and confidence again is much more important than symptom analysis. Understanding why a problem has occurred now often helps explain other difficulties too – a long-standing feud, a problem of jealousy or dislike, the reason for not trying or ever entering a competitive situation.

4   Having clarified the underlying reasons and most likely trigger-factors, work out an acceptable solution which is both realistic and acceptable for the immediate crisis. You may need help to clarify these solutions particularly if your perspectives are narrow or you cannot see a way out of the immediate difficulty. Visualise the best, most positive solution, make it work and a reality. Remember also that other people

have their problems too and that your difficulty is not in total isolation from theirs. Once a solution can clearly be envisaged, there is usually rapid relief from any overwhelming tension or pressure, even if the intermediate steps to change are not yet clear.

5   Visualise the desired positive state clearly. Keep negative thoughts away while building more positive confident self-imagery and outcome. See yourself as you want to be in a particular area, but always take into account the feelings and needs of others involved, at the same time. In your visualised solution look after their needs as much as your own.

6   Keep talking – but not just in a dreary, repetitive, obsessional or draining way. Talk with interest and feeling, taking a real interest in others as you expand. Talk with them, and try to help them with their problems. As you talk listen more. Start to make your talking and thinking a closer reflection of you. Start living, enjoying and expressing life again. Above all start giving caring and feeling for others.

7   Understand why you are in your present situation at this particular time and your own vulnerability as well as your needs. In

general too much tension has built up within you and often because of you. Perhaps early, unresolved or unaccepted problems, have broken through the surface again, triggered off by accumulated stress or a recent hurt. They have usually never been fully dealt with over the years so that any frustration can reactivate them. The least change may sometimes trigger-off a whole chain of pent-up responses which needed release over months or years. Suddenly the mind discharges itself, in a violent frightening reaction and the display of feelings leaves one breathless or feeling like a collapsed house of cards. Whenever accumulated feelings within the psychological or communications system are excessive, panic, pain, palpitations, fainting or tension are common and add to existing uncertainties.

8 It is this emergence of you – as blocked feelings and emotional reactions coming to the surface or symptoms, which creates anxiety and fear. Fear may be present because of the strength of a reaction seemingly unfamiliar and a threat to security. Usually the only threat is to old familiar patterns, and staying in control or on the touch line. Physical reactions are less easily understood at the time, but they do provide an important outlet to tension and depression when the psychological outlets are blocked.

9   As much as possible stay in touch with your
own unique creative-inspirational depths, to
give a more overall perspective. See life
more than just a psychological hurt, a
humiliation or anger response. Pain and disappointment are superficial reactions and
hide the real depths and realities. An
apparent hurt can, with insight, be seen as
one of life's more valuable lessons and
learning experience, although at the time it
was only felt as major stress or trauma. At
the time perhaps, there was also total
inability to respond or to appreciate the
value of the experience other than in the
negative.

10 All life is a learning, an unfolding and a
development. Some hardship and pain are
essential to every life and growth, because
they are part of a freeing and a liberating
from the past, an important stepping-stone
to other depths and development.
Understand that your breakdown is also a
healthy reaction, rather than something
only negative and destructive because it
gives the potential to change, resolve, and
come to terms with an otherwise static area.
The reason you have a breakdown is
because you need it in some way and its
value lies in helping you to new learning,
new adjustments and new perspectives. The
time which a breakdown takes is invaluable
time, not only to think, re-appraise, understand and to know yourself better, but also

time to grow, to express and especially time to change.

11 Think of a breakdown as *your* time to find yourself. See it as an outcome and a preventative. It gives you a breathing space so that life can go on again. Always clarify the true perspectives between the more obvious fears and tensions and the broader deeper positive potentials within you. Getting to grips with a problem is getting to grips with yourself. Aim to get to the 'other side' of a problem, but do so calmly. Take your time so that you can grow-out and learn from the breakdown. Don't hurry too much. This can be the start of a new life, of new beginnings for you. With hindsight, a more mature, new positive approach to life and others is possible. Concentrate on being more you, expressing yourself more openly and authentically saying what you mean and feel, expressing who you are now.

12 In a crisis sit tight, be patient, don't panic or rush, but don't sit on the fence either. Take a position which you most clearly feel, and then express your feelings and views. Be as strong and as spontaneous as you feel at the time, but don't be too intellectual or seeking after reasons. Aim for spontaneity of self, of feelings and ideas so that your real identity can emerge. During an acute breakdown you may get caught up in acute emotion

giving them too much importance and significance. Try to free your thinking from these acute conflicts, and set your mind towards more overall thinking and broader view-points. But also avoid being remote, theoretical, cut-off or isolated at any time.

13 Learn to let the unconscious decide the whys and wherefores. The inspirational you has infinite resolution and healing powers. Combine a relaxed ease with help from friends and helpers. Develop new areas of strength, interest and learning. Make this your *best* experience, not your worst, a turning point, an opening of new doors and pathways. In general be more optimistic and positive about yourself and especially towards others. See the present breakdown as a crisis but not more than that. Especially avoid prejudging yourself or others. To-morrow will be a different day from today, setting different experiences and problems with a new potential for change. Allow life to unfold, and to have its expressions also. Don't keep a tight lid on yourself, rather experience the whole of life's seasons as they come, with interest, joy, gratitude and humility.

Chapter nineteen

On the Best Approach to Localised or Specific Emotional Problems

It is not at all uncommon for the 'well-balanced' adult, with a happy home relationship, a satisfying job and success in their work to nevertheless have some degree of minor emotional difficulty.

Anxiety or tension may only occur with certain people, or in specific social situations causing apprehension. In all other situations and aspects, life is not a problem and pressures and demands can be coped with in an adequate, easy-going, relaxed way.

Such special problem areas are usually familiar patterns, present over the years since childhood or the early teens. Typical examples are hand-shaking or tremor when holding a glass in a social gathering, or carrying a tray into a meeting. Fear of being 'caught short' in a bus or tube is common, or anxiety about sudden diarrhoea, or fainting at a supermarket check-out point in the heat. There may be fears too of travelling, especially on motorways or flying.

Such reactions are known to be irrational, and are often joked or talked about within the family. They have usually never required formal treatment from a doctor. The tendency is to laugh them off and indeed this is a sensible way of approaching them. But they can also be a cause of anxiety and for that reason alone they need to be resolved. Tears and emotional reactions may centre around new, strange situations or where others are felt to be better or made superior in some way. The typical anxiety-situation may also be associated with pleasure and excitement – a holiday, or a visit from friends. If severe, travelling and all new situations may be avoided which causes guilt or deprivation.

Blushing in company, the inability to sleep or relax in a new situation, irregular bowel functioning in a different environment, are other problem areas and minor inhibitions. Ease and naturalness in a social gathering, being able to agree or disagree with tact, to lightly volley a remark or comment are the other areas which become inhibited. Another specific fear is being dominated by an overpowering parental figure – perhaps a mother-in-law, but it could equally be a daughter-in-law who is felt to pose the threat.

Relationships with men or women, where there are sexual or emotional undertones can sometimes be a problem. There may be doubts about coping with such emotions in a social setting. Sometimes there is a fear of supermarkets, of taking something without paying, but there is no conscious impulse to steal or a need for it. For others, there is always a sense of being on the defensive, a fear of being stopped or questioned, which is not based on a reality and is unlikely to occur. Self-confidence and self-trust may become undermined, following an acute illness or a grief reaction where much of life is avoided because of sadness or guilt.

All of these quite localised areas of fear or tension are illogical. They may have existed mildly for many years, limiting activity and spontaneity in certain aspects. Sometimes, there was a clear-cut trauma which explains the symptoms clearly. A woman of sixty could not sleep without a light since being widowed. There had been a similar problem in childhood, with a paralysing fear of the dark at the age of four or five. Her extremely happy, but very dependent maritial relationship, had totally covered up all infantile anxieties and these were only re-activated some 60 years later as part of the grief experience, leading to a temporary revival of infantile fears.

Another common and localised symptom is a fear of falling or collapsing, of getting into a fear state. Loss of control is dreaded because it has actually occurred or because it has been known and seen to happen to someone else. In this way fear, embarrassment or a sense of vulnerability is induced and never grown out of in later years. Jealousy and suspicion are other areas of insecurity which can equally cause pain, anguish and unhappiness. The real origins of jealousy, lie in childhood, and only later becoming localised or centred around a particular relationship or conviction.

Guidelines to Overcoming Localised Areas of Emotional Difficulty

1 First clarify the patterns of any localised symptoms, then try to understand their true meaning and function. See where and how they limit you now, and how much fuller life would be without them. Accept that like everyone else you have areas of weakness and vulnerability. Also that these create blockages to greater satisfaction in life.

2 Realise that such limitation-areas are fixed, habitual patterns, ways of controlling both yourself and others. They are also inappropriate to you, as an adult, because they are rooted in phantasy and no longer

represent reality. The repetitive replay of such fears, not only gives them an outlet, but it also retains them and prevents their release.

3 Try to unravel and de-code any residual patterns of neurotic behaviour you still cling to, their aims and unconscious gains. Attack the puzzle indirectly rather than by a direct intellectual, analytic onslaught.

Dreams and sudden chance associations are the most helpful ways to insight. Keep a pen and paper by you at all times and note them down as they occur to you. If not written down and recorded immediately, they will be quickly forgotten, as the unconscious attempts to obliterate them.

4 Make a detailed note of any meaning or links that occur to you, and always record them in detail. Play the unconscious at its own game by suddenly and spontaneously, 'turning the tables', going into a feared area like a supermarket without warning. In this way you give the unconscious no time to prepare its spectres of fear and anxiety. Develop chance associations, doodles and jottings into insights and understanding, glimpses into your personal reality.

5   Make your unconscious work for you. Don't
    work for it, or let it be the master of your
    ship, controlling you and life's adventure.

6   Work on these insights over a period of
    months, not trying too hard, or making a
    'thing' of it. In this way you will slowly come
    to recognize the major themes and can alter,
    soften or change them as their intensity is
    lessened. One of the most positive signs is
    humour and laughter – at your own
    expense. When you can recognize a
    situation or aspect of your behaviour and
    see why it has occurred or is trying to recur,
    you may also see the funny side of your own
    behaviour. In this way you can balance the
    insecurity threat with a smile or joke.
    Where humour anticipates unconscious
    patterns, you will inevitably be less
    anxious, because you have recognised the
    triggers and mechanisms which were set for
    yet another emotional replay. Insight has
    the edge on the unconscious once insight
    and understanding are present and this is
    what creates change and cure.

7   Laughter is one of life's best medicines for
    any emotional situation. When you can see
    humour, you are also in balance and
    perspective rather than serious, grim or
    rigid. Humour puts unconscious threats to
    flight. The neurotic self, aims to make each
    contact, or relationship fit its own

assumptions and certainties of the past. It opposes change, experience and development. Relaxed humour can balance neurotic drives, however entrenched and determined the patterns.

8 In general, localised symptoms can be resolved within a short period provided you work at them with imagination and humour. They must however be approached with lightness and ease. In this way you will be supporting your creative aspects, opening up healing channels as well as stimulating better emotional balance.

Chapter twenty

Chronic Emotional Problems. How to Cope and Resolve Them

A chronic psychological difficulty is also a positive attempt by the body to adjust and to find a balance. Such problems are a compromise between the wish to contain or maintain an established attitude or position and the desire for change and resolution. There is always a healthy part of the self which is not imprisoned within the nucleus of a chronic problem, and this undistorted self, the germ of health, gives the initiative, drive and potential for health and change.

The roots of a chronic difficulty usually go back in time over many years – sometimes to attitudes and fears which have been clung to since childhood. Over-sensitivity and anxiety may also be traced back through the parents or grandparents, with any eventual problem, the product of hereditary, environment, trauma and suggested or imposed patterns.

The aim in all chronic psychological illness is to perpetuate a former, usually infantile satisfaction, pattern or attitude and to avoid the challenge of the present. There may have been acute problems and crises over the years, which were never fully resolved or worked-through in an adult way. In this way a recurrent situation of pressure and tension may have slowly eroded away both confidence and individuality.

When an initial crisis is not dealt with at the time in a reality way, apprehension and tensions tend to develop, because phantasy dominates reality judgements. Often the initial situation was relatively uncomplicated, a confrontation perhaps, or having to say 'no', or to take to stand in a situation of anger or criticism. The occasion itself was not familiar perhaps, easily dealt with at the time, but the need to impose infantile images, treating every situation as if a first day at school, turned a straightforward situation into a threat.

There is a spark of originality in everyone which becomes blocked or lost by rigid, negative attitudes and infantile assumptions. A gap develops between reality needs and emotion, usually of an immature kind associated with the fear of losing control or failure. The gap between present, past feelings, and reality is a constant source of uncertainty.

Where the gap is wide, there may be alienation from reality, with unreal delusional or obsessional phantasies imposed onto the present, with blockage of insight and understanding.

Where a psychotic unreal element is present, with conviction beyond doubt and perceptual disturbances, then professional help may be required to help regain insight. A lay person is unlikely to have the skills to help but this always depends upon the particular individual, their experience, sincerity and sensitivity. Help is also needed to explore blocks in perception, as well as denied or suppressed areas, to see why these occur and how they are still being maintained. A distorted interpretation of reality makes it difficult to respond appropriately and adds to existing problems.

Guidelines to Resolving Chronic Psychological Problems

Spend part of each day in quiet reflection and pause. Don't allow obsessional, absorbing, dominating or negative thoughts to influence you. Try to remain without conviction or conclusion at the time. Be still, listen to your regular quiet breathing, in contact with your creative sources, the changing seasons, the universe and your position and significance within it. See that in a small way you too contribute to the overall totality and that all nature is change, movement and energy.

Even the most solid states are in a state of flux and alteration, however imperceptible the movements and change. The aim of every chronic illness is to prevent insight and awareness because they lead to growth and change.

Try to see who you are at present, where you are in your development and what you are clinging to from the past. Be more honest about your situation and the people involved with you. See life as a whole with your role, the cast and actors, as part of the theatre of life. Clarify which stituations you turn into a threat. See any specific repetitive preoccupations. When obsessional attitudes are common, see why you cling to them and how they throw you off course.

Family background or an earlier illness, may be important. You may have never been well since a particular illness, vaccination, or perhaps following a miscarriage or operation. You may need help and specific treatment to stimulate development in these areas where there is blockage. Homoeopathy often helps when a psychological condition has clearly developed following an illness or physical intervention of some kind.

Where there is insight and understanding into a chronic problem, then outside help is not so essential. Insight means understanding and clearer perceptions of the underlying reasons behind a particular problem or chronic state of mind, and the role you play in perpetuating and clinging to it. It also implies understanding the reasons for a problem and accepting at least some responsibility for its chronicity.

Awareness, concern and feelings for others may have been limited over the years affecting change, maturity and cure. Try to take much more of a positive step outside yourself and greater responsibility for any problems. In this way you can begin to both grow and resolve them.

Often the only major barrier to cure is yourself. See where and how best to start. Particularly look at areas of conviction, or where you are self-centred and not enough is given-out to others. Make sure that you are not pushing people away from you by aggressive or negative attitudes. If you can already accept and respond to this level of thinking, this is a positive sign. Start to look more at your own roles and attitudes and less at what others have done, or how they have limited or hurt you.

Begin seeing, observing and understanding by looking more at yourself and how you are with others. Note how well you listen and respond. Physical symptoms are often the sign of a blocked, withdrawn self, especially in chronic conditions. Start to look more closely at physical problems too, and see if they are not also the hieroglyphics of a repressed, blocked self. If so, see how you can begin to loosen-up and unblock in these areas also.

Once you develop this inner looking – how you are in the present and less dominated by the past, you can begin to be less controlling and magical in your thinking, more able to make shifts and changes of attitudes. Work through each personal difficulty in detail and be certain that you understand how it relates to problems in the present. See how recurrent old patterns and attitudes affect your interpretation of the present and your behaviour in the now. Get back to the roots of difficulties, not by withdrawing from others, or being over-preoccupied with causes, as this may only reinforce old patterns and attitudes again. Learn from feelings, apprehensions, phobias, dreams, doodling and phantasy. Confront every phobic situation by clearly demonstrating that the risks and fears are not in the actual situation, but only in the feelings you project into it.

If none of the above suggestions makes sense or are helpful and you are still convinced your problems are 'different', due solely to others, consider working for a time with a skilled, therapist or counsellor. Focus initially on one or two areas only. Find someone you like and can relate to, who will see you regularly as a person in a therapeutic, non-judgemental way. In this way you can work together as a team at blocks and difficulties and find a better approach and answer to them. With this sort of teamwork you can also expand and extend as a person, not only reducing tension but finding greater happiness as you grow and can give out more to others.

Chapter twenty-one

Psychosis

Psychosis may be acute or chronic. In acute cases there is a disturbance of perception of reality, the primitive-thinking unconscious with its omnipotent logic, taking over reality appraisal. In this way the world as we experience it, comes to reflect a stream of unconscious phantasy, the inner psychological systems and defences, rather than an evolving outer present. The unconscious takes over the whole surface area of perception and reality interpretation so that it is seen and experienced in much the same way as a dream. This reversal of normality disturbs perceptual input and creates confusion. Because reality-appraisal is disturbed, and inverted, the unconscious processes are felt to be outer reality rather than inner instinct, fear, assumption and wish-fulfilment.

In this way unconscious phantasies become increasingly dominant and actual experiences more remote from perception, judgement and balanced understanding.

Phantasy and imagined experiences of reality are felt to be real statements of fact rather than mirroring fear and phantasy. As the imagery breaks through into consciousness, both inner and outer psychological realities become intermingled. Every sensory experience reflects a magical assumption rather than a true external world of relationships that can be responded and related to.

With psychological reality reversed, and phantasy experienced as coming from outside, a delusional reality occurs. Threatening ideas, events and feelings are pushed away defensively, only to be re-experienced as if thrust back again. The most intimate, personal secret thoughts are felt to be known and talked about by others. Vulnerability comes from a complete breakdown of the normal psychological barriers between a conscious ego and unconscious wishes. As the dividing barrier becomes permeable to every phantasy and idea, there are felt to be no defences, against attack, criticism or manipulation by others.

All of this makes for feelings of fragility and fragmentation, and of living on the surface or through others.

Sometimes it seems as if other people's thoughts are put inside the mind, that their words are in control and directing the individual. Essentially, the person with a psychotic problem feels in bits, scattered and defenceless, unable to get themselves properly together. There is depression and a profound sense of being different, most of all – apart from others. Life is experienced as a kaleidoscope of bits of thought, feeling, imagery and ideas – exciting and fascinating at times, but mainly threatening and isolating. This is particularly common in schizophrenia, the acute form of psychosis of young adults. The basic attempt in all psychosis is to ward-off reality, pain and rejection by making it fragmented or non-existent, but a fragmented reality is also a fragmented self. Yet every psychological experience has its positive side too, however hidden and there are attempts at a healthy, self-realisation and re-integration occurring at the same time as fragmentation. To touch rock-bottom and the extremes of a psychotic experience, may be necessary for the individual to re-emerge with greater sensitivity, awareness and new depths and breadths of perception. In this way psychosis can also be a growth, a learning and a journey into the ultimates of self and not just a disintegrative, purely negative experience.

Exercises to Help Psychotic Problems

1   If you have a psychotic problem, you also are under the influence of non-reality delusional thinking. It is not at all easy to correct this by staying alone in isolation. Avoid any tendency to stay hidden away and alone from sharing contacts. Talk with others and explain your ideas, how you think, see and perceive the world. Listen how others also see and understand the same situation as yourself. Make corrections in understanding whenever you suspect distortion and ask your friends to help you with this. Try to make any 'private' areas much more open and shared. Keep meaningful talking and discussion to a maximum and avoid being alone with your thoughts all the time. In general be more direct, keep living with others, sharing any ideas, thoughts and phantasy out in the open with them.

2   Become more involved in a physical sport or activity which brings you into contact with others. This may vary from table-tennis, cricket to swimming. Counter-balance tendencies to be too cerebral, analysing and intellectual by physical exercise and activity. Choose something near to home, where you can exercise at least three times weekly. Try not to miss it and enjoy the game, contacts and activity.

3   In general think less and experience and enjoy more. Live as much as you can in the moment, in the now, not in the past or future. Continue work and studies, as well as your hobbies or interests. Discuss any aspects that seems odd or peculiar, to counteract tendencies to distort and alter reality. If this happens, stand back from the convictions for a time and try to see them more in keeping with actuality, keeping ideas to the now and reality.

4   Try to recognize delusional beliefs and misinterpretations for what they are – attempts to distort, undermine and take flight from contact or closeness from fear of being overwhelmed. When delusional thoughts come up – recognize them as such, don't act on them, or be deviated by them. Continue strictly at work and in your relationships along a strict reality course, developing, extending and broadening your experiences. Once a delusional idea is recognized it can be let go of and will eventually diminish and disappear because understanding and recognition lessens its influence and power. At the same time you will have grown in strength and insight and be less vulnerable in the future.

Chapter twenty-two

Schizophrenia

In schizophrenia, or psychosis of young adults,
thoughts, conceptions and ideas are exploded
into fragments, each with its narrow viewpoint
of understanding, and interpretation. Each
fragment may be re-experienced through
another person, because inter-personal
boundaries are thin and weakened by the
illness, causing confusion as to where self ends
and others begin. Because of the breakdown of
normal divisions and proportions, there is
distortion of body image, causing a foreign,
unreal sense of identity as if, controlled or
influenced by others. Ideas, thoughts, and
impulses are thought to come from, or to be
inside other people. There is a sense of living in,
or through others, sometimes of not existing.
Because the boundaries between self and others
are so weak the actions, gestures, and speech of
others can be experienced as coded, undermining or influencing adding to an overall
sense of confusion or of being in 'bits'.

Delusional beliefs and convictions are attempts to rationalise and understand confused thought and body imagery. Attempts may be made to deny the whole experience of psychological reality by extruding all feelings into others, leaving a painless void inside. But fear and panic can never be totally ousted because of the overwhelming sense of vulnerability which results.

At such moments the schizophrenic feels dead or non-existent. Because of attempts to deny or project the personal self, there is a constant image of living inside or through others, a part of everything seen and heard, but with no solid core or foundation of individuality.

Alienation from the deep and the sensitive, the inspirational-creative self, leads to a sense of loneliness, anguish and guilt. In extreme cases he or she may complain that they have lost or killed their soul. There is loss of all meaning to life, a delusion of having destroyed the beautiful and being condemned to mediocrity, illness, and sometimes even damnation. Such feelings and convictions create an extremely confused, painful and worrying situation, with suspicion and mistrust, adding to alienation and the problem of finding help at an early stage of the illness.

General Guidelines to Schizophrenic Problems and How Best to Approach Them

If you suspect that you may have a schizophrenic problem, or it has already been diagnosed, it is unlikely that you are fully aware of its full range and extent because the illness tends to lessen insight and understanding.

When you are unsure of what is happening, get help and advice from someone you trust — a friend perhaps. Their age is not important. Consider also either a priest, healer, doctor, counsellor or therapist. But don't stay isolated, lost within your phantasies and imagery. You need outside help and positive contacts to support healing and cure. With schizophrenia, you must maximise reality-contacts to counterbalance excessive phantasy imagery and the delusional beliefs which impose their own logic on meaning and experience.

Try to remember also that you are not so different from others, and that you can be understood or express yourself as long as you maintain interest and contact. It is important to maintain relationships and to develop them for balance and healthy psychological growth. The re-uniting with lost, fragmented aspects of self is vital as these can never be permanently maintained or denied outside the self without serious consequences. These denied aspects of yourself and feeling must be acknowledged and owned however disturbing their thoughts and associations, or the sense of vulnerability. In schizophrenia there is a tendency to constantly project and fragment every disturbing aspect of life into others, or other situations which makes everything seem familiar and *deja vu*, but it is a very weakening process for the individual at the same time.

Laing has emphasised the explorative, positive learning aspect of schizophrenia and that the illness can be a first step towards re-discovery of self and identity. In general keep as external and as close to others as you can, especially to people you like and feel positive about. But don't spend your day with negative, critical people, who may try to maintain your sickness, or delay insight and change.

Consider contacting the Samaritans if you are unsure where to go for help. But try to talk and relate to at least someone, and maintain the contact, ideally with a person of your own age. Don't rely on the telephone, other than to make an initial contact. You need to see and look at the person you are relating to. A member of your family may be of enormous help, but in general make a contact with someone outside the family too, who is prepared to listen and give a balanced opinion.

With schizophrenia, you are likely to need professional advice and guidance at some time. This may be from a doctor, trained counsellor or sensitive healer but find *someone* you like, feel comfortable with, and expecially someone you can relate and talk to and who is prepared to listen.

In general, a psychotic problem such as schizophrenia is too much for you to resolve alone, when under pressure and in isolation. The schizophrenic process can be a stepping stone to learning and growth however odd, bizarre and incomprehensible it seems at the time. Always maximise reality contacts and involvements, at work and social levels, so that a re-integrative sharing and dialogue can begin with others.

In curing schizophrenia, the fragmenting, projecting process must always be reversed by the patient with a greater acceptance of self and feelings. This is essential in order to regain a sense of self and identity. Once the trend from omnipotence and delusional invulnerability has been reversed to more mundane human frailty, then cure is also possible.

Chapter twenty-three

Manic-Depressive Problems

Manic-depressive mood swings are severe mood disturbances leading to illness and a varying degree of incapacity. There is a disturbance in depth, the causes obscure, often inherited. The outcome or course of the illness is also uncertain and sometimes a chronic course develops. A break or split occurs between reality-appraisal and phantasy imagery so that most of the time, the individual functions at a delusional level which leads to delusional beliefs, excitement and over-activity. Hypochondriacal or irrational behaviour occurs as the instinctual drives are wound up into a frenzy or manic state, which take over all activity. Relaxation, judgement and balance are all undermined by the intrusion of raw, intense emotion into the physical, which becomes driven by excesses of energy in all of its rhythms and functioning.

The psychological ego may develop a chronic state of pressure and over-activity, wound up and over-inflated by feelings which it can no longer contain. It is these pressures which lead to the manic-depressive picture of intermittent over-activity and mania, or profound depression.

Any former psychological hurt, shock, or trauma, may reactivate itself and fester, stirring-up old scars, resentments and wounds in a damaging way. When the underlying shock has been profound, a division can occur between the reality-perceiving self and its deeper inspirational-creative roots, causing an unbalancing effect. Alienation combined with an over-pressurised ego causes excessive energy to be generated which is later released as mood disturbance. As the abnormal psychological energy over-spills into physical channels, there is a surge of drive, physical well-being and energy. The absence of fatigue causes insomnia and continual over-activity. Such drive feels both uncontrollable and exhilarating, but also frightening, like a lorry rolling downhill without brakes. In a low mood, the opposite happens and the least effort is agony and a tremendous effort, because there is no available energy, except for lying in bed, hour after hour to try and recuperate.

Once a high manic phase has been generated, it is inevitably followed by a 'low', depressive one. The abrupt change in mood and the delusional certainty, creates conviction and guilt as well as panic, because judgement and control are undermined.

When objective thinking occurs, it is usually too 'heady' and speculative. Because delusional ideas must at the same time be rationalised and acceptable, external reality is distorted to make the phantasies seem logical and coherent. Distortions of reality and people, their reactions and motivations, eventually undermines all relationships and judgement, putting the individual, family and finances at risk because of errors of judgement and assumption-behaviour.

Exercises to Diminish Manic-Depressive Problems

1   Work first to clarify your mood swings, how and when they occur and any 'trigger' factors which precipitate them. Then practise daily as in the chapter on mood swings with periods of deep relaxation. Repeat these for 15-20 minutes three times daily, continuing the practice during periods of high or low mood swing, less frequently at other times.

2   Develop insight and understanding into the underlying causes during a quiescent phase. Once a period of over-activity or depression develops it is not always possible to correct or understand it because of loss of insight. So do as much homework as possible about any causative factors during a period of calm and balance.

3   When in a 'high' phase, try to recognize it and learn clues to its existence. The commonest, is usually a surge of drive and energy, a lack of need for sleep. Take no decisions, especially financial ones at this stage. Eat regularly and slowly, and try to be relaxed and easy until it passes. In a 'low' depressive phase, don't retreat to bed, but be reasonably active. Get out of the house, walking each day for periods of $\frac{1}{2}$-1 hour. Try not to take major decisions while in either a low depressive phase or when over-charged and excitable.

Chapter twenty-four

Physical Health and Psychological Balance

Every positive aspect of life is the outcome of harmony and balance, and this is also true for relationship between the physical and the psychological. Both depend to some extent upon the other for health, perspective and vitality, and where one is predominant, it quickly undermines the other. The excessive metabolic activity that occurs when the thyroid gland is over-active, provokes restlessness, palpitations and weight loss but also causes anxiety, insomnia and exhaustion. In a similar way physical health, resistance and physiological functioning are directly linked to feelings and can be reduced or stimulated by emotional health.

Physical health is supported by:-

1 Sound constitutional and hereditary factors with adequate physical reserves and available vitality.

2 Relaxed mental attitudes, free from excessive pressures and stress, generally enhance physical health.

Negative attitudes drain body reserves causing malaise and weakness, with an increased predisposition to physical disease. Chronic stress states are responsible for a great deal of the common accidents and injuries which daily occur, for accident-proneness and the self-destructive behaviour or negligence which cost every government millions of pounds yearly. Failure to relax, because of chronic tension results in many of the sport and activity injuries which occur and some of these can also be incapacitating for long periods.

3 A varied interesting diet which contains a balanced proportion of protein, fat, carbohydrate and fibre with adequate vitamin and mineral content. Raw food and fresh fruit are also essential daily for health, whatever the age of the individual.

4   Moderation of the social-addictive habits, especially tea and coffee drinking, smoking and alcohol, supports health. All undermine when taken to excess. Every synthetic drug and chemical is a potential danger and should be taken for a minimum period and with caution. The regular, long-term use of synthetics is not recommended. Expecially avoid the prolonged, habitual use of aperients for constipation; analgesics for pain; antibiotics for minor infections; sprays and lozenges for minor, recurrent conditions. Hormones, sedatives, stimulants and tranquillisers should be kept to minimal amounts and only used when strictly necessary. Every synthetic can be potentially harmful in the long term, ultimately reducing health, physical vitality and often depressing mood and confidence.

5   Graded regular exercise, depending upon age and fitness without strain or excess, and within the limits of individual fatigue, increases vitality, resistance and stamina. Excessive, sudden effort, without training or preparation, is dangerous and should be avoided. Regular exercise has far greater overall value than sudden, erratic bouts leading to exhaustion. An on-going sexual relationship gives a balanced stimulation and relaxation to both physical and psychological outlets and should be continued in a regular rhythmic way throughout life.

6 Adequate sleep is essential at every age. Tension and fear undermine sleep and are the common causes of a jaded vitality and fatigue. The prolonged use of sedatives tends to make natural sleep impossible because of dependency problems and they should be kept minimal or used for short periods only.

7 Hygiene and natural elimination through the skin is essential and desirable, but should not be excessive or obsessional. In a similar way the bowels should be regular and controlled by diet, but not become a preoccupation. The urinary system must also function regularly for health, with adequate liquid intake, according to climate, age, exercise and humidity, but excessive fluid intake is rarely recommended.

8 Where there is a 'cerebral' problem of too much thinking, too much worrying and too much 'going on' in the mind this should be balanced, by a regular, graded, physical activity depending upon age and general fitness. Everyone can walk or learn to swim but not everyone can play tennis or jog, especially on a hot day. Be sensible in your approach and if in doubt ask your doctor for a check-up before you begin.

If you are over-weight, diet and reduce to your to the optimum level for your age and height. When underweight, change your dietary intake, increasing both protein and carbohydrate, as well as the quality of your food in general. If you are too tense, practise deep relaxation and try to 'let go' of problems in a physical way. Let tension and worry almost melt away as you relax. One of the popular meditation techniques may be of help, as long as it feels right for you and does not in itself create problems or stress. Try the visualisation exercises suggested and be as creative, imaginative and original as you can in your relaxation.

You should not be thinking about your problems throughout the day. If you are, then you are over-involved with them, and you need extra time for more relaxation and letting go. You should be able to look at all difficulties in an overall way. Approach problem-solving with more confidence as you separate-out the realities, and what needs to be done from what you fear may occur. Never let fears of what might be dominate your thinking. Concentrate on what you can do *now*, and the next step at a reality level which you are can accomplish. Don't think beyond that or stimulate anxiety.

Chapter twenty-five

On the Best Ways to Prevent Breakdown and Strain. How to Limit Nervousness when Under Pressure

Learn to relax and to release pressure and strain as it is happening – not before or after. The best way to relax is to flop out flat on the floor, in a quiet darkened room, letting everything 'float'. If this is not physically possible, flop out on a chair, but let go of all thinking and body tension, especially let go of any problems. Lie, or sit quietly, breathing regularly and quietly, distancing yourself from the immediate problems while you relax. You should be absorbed in your relaxation, totally within it and not still be thinking about any difficulties. Formal meditation is not essential unless you prefer it, but let this be a period of letting go and try not to allow interruptions to occur at this time. Unplug the telephone and let others know you want to be quiet. Warm baths relax, but they should not be too hot. Saunas are tonic and stimulating but can sometimes be over-stimulating, even dangerous when prolonged.

Never take a hot bath or shower when you are hot, sweating, or exhausted. The heat at this time is a strain on the heart and circulation. Once you start to relax both body and mind, repeat the pattern regularly. Sit still without searching, seeking or trying. The aim is to increase awareness of you as a total being, your depths and inspirational links so that stress, fear and problems can be put back into perspective. Don't try to be or to do anything, even to be aware. Awareness is already there if you will listen for it. Be still, listen, and let your thoughts come up and go down. Don't hang on to them or be critical. Be much more tolerant of your thoughts and of yourself, seeing them as children in need of attention, but not taking you over. Nothing should deviate you from quiet calm. Once thoughts are perceived in this way, they gradually lessen and diminish, as long as they are not pushed under, suppressed or denied. Accept each thought or worry as a part of yourself – but don't let them dominate your mind or your essential being.

Practise frequent breaks from work and worry, leaving problems behind you while you relax, meditate or just enjoy. If you cannot sleep or be quiet, meditate and practise stillness. Take time off from thinking, to give yourself more space as an individual to emerge and to grow. In this way relaxation puts problems and pressures back into perspective, into overall priority and significance.

It is never healthy or balanced to be over-dominated by one particular psychological process or excess of feeling because they impose their own values and impressions upon the whole and cause distortion. Fear should not be allowed to impose upon the rest of your mind, particularly upon quiet, intuitive thought as it induces a negative pattern. In the same way, the intellectual processes should not dominate flexible thinking and awareness, to make it too coherent and logical, so that feelings are denied.

Further Insights for Relaxation

Aim to get into balance by regular periods of rest, distancing yourself from tension and immediate problems. Be more easy and rational, less dominated or taken over by a particular area of difficulty. Try to see how others might see, react, feel and resolve the immediate stresses and realise that there is more than one way to look at them and to resolve their demands. Get an overall perspective, realising that problems are neither as unique, nor as devastating as you make them to be. Separate yourself from jealousy, fear, envy, rage, resentment and revenge and avoid acting impetuously or precipitately. This is not spontaneity or responding in the moment, but more a reaction of fear and fright, being hasty, trying to rush away rather than finding a solution to the pressures and challenges.

Look back at similar, past problem areas with hindsight. But don't hold 'post mortems'. Project yourself forward in time as well as backwards and look back at yourself as you are now, to see if it is positive or needs an adjustment.

Perspective and an overall position are important to responding in the present. Feelings of defeat, depression and despair are usually repetitive patterns rather than responses to a difficulty. Look back at your overall changes over the past ten years and recall how you resolved a seemingly insolvable crisis during that period. Look forward also towards new aims and the directions you envisage in the next decade. See yourself already there and look back at yourself as you are now seeing the present, doubts and problems as part of life, growth and experience. See each problem as a potential turning point which you would not have missed on your developmental experience.

Look at an immediate crisis from all sides. It is likely that it will seem less of an overwhelming disaster and that there are several approaches possible. When you let go of a crisis, stand back from it, there is every chance that it can be seen in a more relaxed way and resolved as part of problem-solving generally.

If an existing strain seems part of a repetitive pattern or trend you are probably repeating obsessional closed attitudes to ward-off reality as you imagine it to be. Being continually 'caught-up' in a contrived psychological situation of your own making is an attempt to live in a known familiar past however painful, to deny and avoid unfolding issues and challenges.

It is rarely helpful to get irritated or worked-up over a problem and where there is a threat to security, over-reacting usually hides vulnerability and anxiety. Tension is always the outcome of personal blockage and if you are too tense, you are not in an optimum position to understand, or creatively resolve your problem areas.

Chapter twenty-six

Basic Guidelines to Building Healthy Protective Ego Strengths and Flexibility

1 Build a wide variety of experience, closeness and contacts with others. Do this through friends, colleagues and family, sharing and giving out as much of your feelings and ideas as possible. In this way there can be joy, an enriching of others as well as your own development.

The elderly need the young for their freshness, hope, spontaneity, and unspoiled perceptions. The young need the elderly for their wisdom, experience and what they can teach and share. Men and women naturally need each other, not only to combat distortion but to soften areas of assumption, and rigidity about each other.

2 Experience new contacts, meetings, situations and challenges without prejudgement or anxiety about an outcome. In this way you can understand yourself better and develop experience and awareness. Only a wide variety of situations and contacts gives confidence as the natural outcome of being and doing.

3 Accept life's challenges and problems as a stimulus for change. Welcome difficulty as a potential for growth.

4 Expand existing interests in greater depth, and become an expert in one field of interest. Greater knowledge gives greater understanding, a degree of real excellence and real confidence. Deepen satisfactions by giving more to others. Find joy and enthusiasm by sharing, leading to greater involvement and a deepening of closeness, caring and insight.

5 Openness, spontaneity, interest and giving, encourages responses from others, so that there is a return of interest, new learning and confidence. In this way you help others to grow, creating life and growth. Friendships develop from talking and sharing with interest, and feeling, so that a truly creative original development occurs.

Gain deeper satisfactions by giving. Warmth and appreciation are the natural outcome of giving to others.

In this way you will be living more broadly and in a more balanced way. Fears, self-protection, self-interest, phantasy and threats can be minimised by such contacts especially where there is generosity, trust and sharing. Outer caring develops inner appreciation and joy helping to balance inner fears and insecurity which lead to illness. As outer interests grow, so inner strengths develop as an inseparable part of contacts, creating closeness, experience and a greater sense of value, worth, appreciation and health.

Index